# VOGUE.KNITTING
# LACE

# VOGUE KNITTING

# LACE

# 40 BOLD & DELICATE KNITS

BY THE EDITORS OF
VOGUE KNITTING MAGAZINE

ROSE CALLAHAN

sixth&springbooks

**sixth&springbooks**

An imprint of Soho Publishing LLC
19 West 21st Street, Suite 601
New York, NY 10010
www.sixthandspring.com

Editor
JACOB SEIFERT

Art Director
IRENE LEDWITH

Book Designer
DANITA ALBERT

Pattern Consultant
CARLA SCOTT

Chief Executive Officer
CAROLINE KILMER

Production Manager
DAVID JOINNIDES

President
ART JOINNIDES

Chairman
JAY STEIN

Library of Congress Cataloging-in-Publication Data

Title: Vogue knitting lace : 40 bold and delicate knits / by the editors of Vogue Knitting Magazine.
Other titles: Vogue knitting international.
Description: First edition. | New York, New York : Sixth&Spring Books, [2021] | Includes index.
Identifiers: LCCN 2021005014 | ISBN 9781970048063 (hardcover)
Subjects: LCSH: Knitted lace—Patterns.
Classification: LCC TT805.K54 V64 2021 | DDC 746.2/26—dc23
LC record available at https://lccn.loc.gov/2021005014

ISBN: 978-1-970048-06-3

Manufactured in China

3 5 7 9 10 8 6 4 2

First Edition

FOLLOW US:

# CONTENTS

ROSE CALLAHAN

# LACE FOR ALL

When discussion turned to publishing another book of *Vogue Knitting* patterns, it seemed all too obvious that lace should be the theme this time around. It is such a beloved technique among us knitters, and for good reason. Knitting a lace project is fun, addictive, and so satisfying as you watch the pattern grow from your needles. Furthermore, some of the most stunning designs to appear in the pages of *Vogue Knitting* have been lace projects that still leave me breathless.

When hearing the word "lace," many immediately conjure up in their minds images of delicate, lightweight shawls worked in the classic intricate patterns we all know and love. While such projects are a prime example and an important part of knitting history, lace is more diverse than many realize. So, when selecting patterns for this collection—which was a difficult task due to the sheer number of gorgeous options—we did our best to include a range of project types, skill levels, and approaches to highlight the endless potential of what lace can be.

From an easy-wear stockinette pullover with a lace yoke (see page 17) to a generously sized wrap with three columns of flowing openwork (see page 55), lace can be a powerful design element. Whether a complex design worked across a large shawl (see page 69) or several simple eyelet repeats (see page 75), lace's effectiveness is not bound by scale or complexity. Worked sparsely across a simple accessory (see page 85) or fearlessly knitted as separate motifs to be joined later (see page 87), lace is limited only by the range of our own imaginations.

This collection of 40 patterns represents some of the most stunning work found in the pages of *Vogue Knitting*, and there is something for every knitter to enjoy. If you are new to or not quite confident with lace, start simple with an accessory or a garment with a lace insert. If you are looking for a challenge, cast on for a large shawl or an intricate pullover. No matter your skill level or personal style, lace is a technique that all can enjoy.

*—Norah Gaughan*
Editor in Chief, VOGUE KNITTING

# ECHO

Perfect for an evening with just a hint of a chill, Lisa Hoffman's bias-knit shawl alternates stripes of cables with their reflection in a delicate lace pattern. You'll slide easily into the rhythm of increasing and decreasing stitches as you work your way across this generously-sized wrap.

## KNITTED MEASUREMENTS
**Width** 21"/53.5cm
**Length (along one side)** 79"/200.5cm

## MATERIALS
• 6 1¾oz/50g balls (each approx 180yd/165m) of **String Yarns** Amalfi (viscose/wool/silk/cashmere) in #728330 Sea Pink (2)
• One size 7 (4.5mm) circular needle, 24"/60cm long, OR SIZE TO OBTAIN GAUGES
• Stitch markers

## GAUGES
• 18 sts and 26 rows to 4"/10cm over St st using size 7 (4.5mm) needle.
• 14 sts and 26 rows to 4"/10cm over lace pat using size 7 (4.5mm) needle.
TAKE TIME TO CHECK GAUGES.

## NOTES
**1)** Though gauge is not critical, work and block a swatch to check gauge and ensure a drapey fabric.
**2)** Slip first stitch of every row knitwise with yarn in back.
**3)** Place markers around 12-st pattern reps, placing new markers and removing previous markers when necessary.
**4)** Lace pattern may be worked from written instructions or chart.
**5)** Circular needle is used to accommodate large number of sts. Do not join.

## STITCH GLOSSARY
**3-st LC** Sl 2 sts to cn and hold to front of work, k1, k2 from cn.
**4-st LC** Sl 2 sts to cn and hold to front of work, k2, k2 from cn.

## SHAWL
Cast on 116 sts.
Purl 1 row on WS.

### Begin Lace Pattern
**Row 1 (RS)** Sl 1, M1, k1, k2tog, yo, k1, *p1, 4-st LC, p1, k3, k2tog, yo, k1; rep from * to last 3 sts, k2tog tbl, k1.
**Row 2 and all WS rows** Sl 1, k the knit sts and p the purl sts and yarnovers to last st, k1.
**Row 3** Sl 1, M1, k1, k2tog, yo, k2, *p1, k4, p1, k2, k2tog, yo, k2; rep from * to last 14 sts, p1, k4, p1, k2, k2tog, yo, k1, k2tog tbl, k1.
**Row 5** Sl 1, M1, k1, k2tog, yo, k3, *p1, 4-st LC, p1, k1, k2tog, yo, k3; rep from * to last 13 sts, p1, 4-st LC, p1, k1, k2tog, yo, k1, k2tog tbl, k1.
**Row 7** Sl 1, M1, p1, k2tog, yo, k4, *p1, k4, p1, k2tog, yo, k4; rep from * to last 12 sts, p1, k4, p1, k2tog, yo, k1, k2tog tbl, k1.
**Row 9** Sl 1, M1, k1, p1, k3, k2tog, yo, k1, *p1, 4-st LC, p1, k3, k2tog, yo, k1; rep from * to last 11 sts, p1, 4-st LC, p1, k2, k2tog tbl, k1.
**Row 11** Sl 1, M1, k2, p1, k2, k2tog, yo, k2, *p1, k4, p1, k2, k2tog, yo, k2; rep from * to last 10 sts, p1, k4, p1, k1, k2tog tbl, k1.
**Row 13** Sl 1, M1, 3-st LC, p1, k1, k2tog, yo, k3, *p1, 4-st LC, p1, k1, k2tog, yo, k3; rep from * to last 9 sts, p1, 4-st LC, p1, k2tog tbl, k1.
**Row 15** Sl 1, M1, k4, p1, k2tog, yo, k4, *p1, k4, p1, k2tog, yo, k4; rep from * to last 8 sts, p1, k4, k2tog tbl, k1.
**Row 17** Sl 1, M1, p1, 4-st LC, p1, k3, k2tog, yo, k1, *p1, 4-st LC, p1, k3, k2tog, yo, k1; rep from * to last 7 sts, p1, 3-st LC, k2tog tbl, k1.
**Row 19** Sl 1, M1, k1, *p1, k4, p1, k2, k2tog, yo, k2; rep from * to last 6 sts, p1, k2, k2tog tbl, k1.

**Row 21** Sl 1, M1, k2, *p1, 4-st LC, p1, k1, k2tog, yo, k3; rep from * to last 5 sts, p1, k1, k2tog tbl, k1.
**Row 23** Sl 1, M1, k3, *p1, k4, p1, k2tog, yo, k4; rep from * to last 4 sts, p1, k2tog tbl, k1.
**Row 24** Rep row 2.
Rep rows 1–24 thirteen times more, then work rows 1–8 once more.
**Next row (RS)** Sl 1, M1, k8, p1, 4-st LC, *p1, k6, p1, 4-st LC; rep from * to last 6 sts, p1, k2, k2tog tbl, k1.

**Next row (WS)** Bind off, dec'ing center sts of each cable as foll: bir off 6 sts, p2tog, bind off previous st, *bind off 10 sts, p2tog, bind previous st; rep from * to end.

FINISHING
Weave in ends. Block to measurements.•

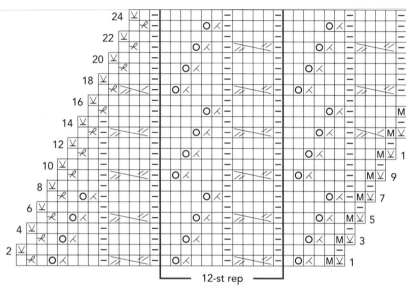

12-st rep

**STITCH KEY**

☐ k on RS, p on WS

– p on RS, k on WS

∨ sl 1 wyib

⊀ k2tog

⊀ k2tog tbl

Ο yo

M M1

3-st LC

4-st LC

# CHÂLE DE LAVANDE

Whether or not you choose a yarn with a bit of shimmer, Wei Wilkens' wrap will leave you entranced. A garter stitch border surrounds the edges of this drapable rectangle while the overall lace pattern is composed of yarnovers and decreases that result in a bewitching series of shapes reminiscent of a classic fleur-de-lis.

## KNITTED MEASUREMENTS
**Width** 24"/61cm
**Length** 70"/178cm

## MATERIALS
• 4  4.2oz/119g hanks (each approx 425yd/389m) of **Anzula Luxury Fibers** Lunaris (superwash merino wool/cashmere/sparkling stellina) in Elephant ( 1 )
• One size 5 (3.75mm) circular needle, 40"/60cm long, OR SIZE TO OBTAIN GAUGE
• Stitch markers

## GAUGE
23 sts and 33 rows to 4"/10cm over lace pat using size 5 (3.75mm) needle.
TAKE TIME TO CHECK GAUGE

## NOTE
**1)** Circular needle is used to accommodate the large number of stitches. Do not join.
**2)** Lace pattern may be worked from written instructions or chart.

## BACKWARD LOOP CAST-ON
**1)** Place a slipknot on the right needle, leaving a short tail. Wrap the yarn from the ball around your left thumb from front to back and secure it in your palm with your other fingers.
**2)** Insert the needle upward through the strand on your thumb.
**3)** Slip this loop from your thumb onto the needle, pulling the yarn from the ball to tighten it. Continue in this way until all the stitches are cast on.

## STITCH GLOSSARY
**ssssk** Sl 3 sts one at a time, k1, pass 3 sl sts over the k1—3 sts dec'd.

## LACE PATTERN

(multiple of 19 sts plus 8)

**Row 1 (RS)** K4, *p1, [yo, ssk] twice, p3, yo, S2KP, yo, p3, [k2tog, yo] twice, p1; rep from * to last 4 sts, k4.

**Row 2** K4, *k1, p4, k9, p4, k1; rep from * to last 4 sts, k4.

**Row 3** K4, *p1, k1, [yo, ssk] twice, p2, k3, p2, [k2tog, yo] twice, k1, p1; rep from * to last 4 sts, k4.

**Row 4** K4, *k1, p5, k2, p3, k2, p5, k1; rep from * to last 4 sts, k4.

**Row 5** K4, *p1, [yo, ssk] 3 times, p1, yo, S2KP, yo, p1, [k2tog, yo] 3 times, p1; rep from * to last 4 sts, k4.

**Row 6** K4, *k1, p6, k5, p6, k1; rep from * to last 4 sts, k4.

**Row 7** K4, *p1, k2tog, yo, p1, [yo, ssk] twice, k3, [k2tog, yo] twice, p1, yo, ssk, p1; rep from * to last 4 sts, k4.

**Row 8** K4, *k1, p2, k2, p9, k2, p2, k1; rep from * to last 4 sts, k4.

**Row 9** K4, *p1, yo, ssk, p2, [yo, ssk] twice, k1, [k2tog, yo] twice, p2, k2tog, yo, p1; rep from * to last 4 sts, k4.

**Row 10** K4, *k1, p2, k3, p7, k3, p2, k1; rep from * to last 4 sts, k4.

**Row 11** K4, *p1, k2tog, yo, p3, yo, ssk, yo, S2KP, yo, k2tog, yo, p3, yo, ssk, p1; rep from * to last 4 sts, k4.

**Row 12** K4, *k1, p2, k4, p5, k4, p2, k1; rep from * to last 4 sts, k4.

**Row 13** K4, *p1, yo, ssk, p4, yo, ssk, k1, k2tog, yo, p4, k2tog, yo, p1; rep from * to last 4 sts, k4.

**Row 14** K4, *k1, p2, k5, p3, k5, p2, k1; rep from * to last 4 sts, k4.

**Row 15** K4, *p1, k2tog, yo, p5, yo, S2KP, yo, p5, yo, ssk, p1; rep from * to last 4 sts, k4.

**Row 16** Rep row 14.

**Row 17** K4, *p1, k1 tbl, p1, k4tog, yo, [k1, yo] 5 times, ssssk, p1, k1 tbl, p1; rep from * to last 4 sts, k4.

**Row 18** K4, *k1, p1 tbl, k1, p13, k1, p1 tbl, k1; rep from * to last 4 sts, k4.

**Row 19** K4, *p1, k1 tbl, p1, k13, p1, k1 tbl, p1; rep from * to last 4 sts, k4.

**Row 20** Rep row 18.

**Rows 21–24** Rep rows 17–20.

**Rows 25–26** Rep rows 17–18.

Rep rows 1–26 for lace pat.

## WRAP

Using backward loop cast-on, cast on 141 sts.
Knit 6 rows.

### Begin Lace Pattern

Rep rows 1–26 of lace pat until piece measures approx 69"/175cm from beg, end with a pat row 16.
Knit 5 rows. Bind off.

## FINISHING

Block gently to measurements. Weave in ends. •

**19-st rep**

## STITCH KEY

☐ k on RS, p on WS

− p on RS, k on WS

Ω k1 tbl on RS, p1 tbl on WS

O yo

⊿ k2tog

⊾ ssk

⅄ S2KP

⊿ k4tog

⊾ ssssk

# PULL JACINTHE

Amy Gunderson's top-down, classic-fit sweater serves delightful details: graceful lace and mini cables embrace the yoke, the silhouette gets a boost from gentle waist shaping, the hem falls below the hips, and subtle statement sleeves are accentuated by a hint of a bell shape.

## SIZES
Small (Medium, Large, 1X, 2X, 3X, 4X).
Shown in size Small.

## KNITTED MEASUREMENTS
**Bust** 36¼ (39¼, 42¼, 45¼, 48¼, 51½, 54½)"/92 (99.5, 107, 115, 123, 130.5, 138.5)cm
**Length** 24½ (25, 25½, 26, 26½, 27, 27½)"/62 (63.5, 64.5, 66, 67.5, 68.5, 70)cm
**Upper arm** 12½ (14, 15½, 17, 18½, 18½, 18½)"/31.5 (35.5, 39.5, 43, 47, 47, 47)cm

## MATERIALS
• 7 (7, 8, 9, 10, 10, 11) 1¾oz/50g balls (each approx 167yd/153m) of **Rozetti/Universal Yarn** Merino Mist (viscose/wool/acrylic) in #106 Drizzle
• Two size 6 (4mm) circular needles, one each 16"/40cm and 24"/60cm long, OR SIZE TO OBTAIN GAUGE
• One size 4 (3.5mm) circular needle, 16"/40cm long
• One set (5) each sizes 4 and 6 (3.5 and 4mm) double-pointed needles (dpn)
• Stitch markers
• Stitch holders
• Cable needle (cn)

## GAUGE
21 sts and 28 rows to 4"/10cm over St st using larger needles.
TAKE TIME TO CHECK GAUGE.

## NOTE
Pullover is worked in the round from the neck down with short-row shaping at the neck.

## SHORT ROW WRAP & TURN (w&t)
on RS row (on WS row)
**1)** Wyib (wyif), sl next st purlwise.
**2)** Move yarn between the needles to the front (back).
**3)** Sl the same st back to LH needle. Turn work. One st is wrapped.
**4)** When working the wrapped st, insert RH needle under the wrap and work it together with the corresponding st on needle.

## STITCH GLOSSARY
**RT (right twist)** K2tog but do not drop sts from needle, knit first st again and allow both sts to drop from needle.
**LT (left twist)** K 2nd st on LH needle through back loop, knit first st on LH needle, allow both sts to drop from needle.
**1/1/1 RC** Sl 1 st to cn and hold to back, RT over next 2 sts on LH needle, k1 from cn.
**1/1/1 LC** Sl 1 st to cn and hold to front, RT over next 2 sts on LH needle, k1 from cn.

## SWEATER
With size 4 (3.5mm) circular needle, cast on 96 sts. Join, taking care not to twist sts, and pm for beg of rnd.
Knit 3 rnds.
**Next rnd** *K1, p1, k1; rep from * around.
Rep last rnd 5 times more.

### Short-Row Neck Shaping
**Note** Rnd begins at center back neck.
**Row 1 (RS)** Work 23 sts in rib as established, w&t.
**Row 2 (WS)** Work 46 sts in rib, w&t.
**Row 3** Work in rib to 3 sts before last wrapped st, w&t.
**Row 4** Work in rib to 3 sts before last wrapped st, w&t.
Rep rows 3 and 4 twice more.
**Row 9 (RS)** Work in rib back to beg of rnd marker.
Change to shorter size 6 (4mm) circular needle and resume working in the rnd as foll:
**Next rnd** Work in rib as established, picking up wraps.
Work 1 rnd more in rib.

**Begin Yoke Chart**

**Note** Change to longer size 6 (4mm) circular needle when necessary.

**Rnd 1** Work 6-st rep 16 times around.

Cont to work chart in this way through rnd 15.

**Rnd 16** Remove beg of rnd marker, sl last st of rnd 15 to LH needle, work rnd 16 to last st, sl last st to RH needle, replace beg of rnd marker.

Cont to work chart through rnd 55—288 sts.

**Note** Increases are worked on either side of "center" st from yoke motif. For all sizes except size Small, place a shaping marker on either side of 8th st of each repeat as shown on chart, slipping these markers on following rnds.

**Next rnd** K31, pm, work rnd 1 of cable panel chart over 5 sts, pm, [k31, pm, work rnd 1 of cable panel over 5 sts, pm] twice, k67, pm, work rnd 1 of cable panel over 5 sts, pm, [k31, pm, work rnd 1 of cable panel over 5 sts, pm] twice, k36.

**Next rnd** Work 5 sts in cable panel as established and knit all other sts.

**For Size Small Only**

Rep last rnd until yoke measures 8"/20.5cm from rnd 1 of yoke chart.

**For Sizes Medium, Large, 1X, and 2X Only**

**Inc rnd** [Work to shaping marker, M1R, sm, k1, sm, M1L] 16 times, work to end—32 sts inc'd.

Cont in pats as established, rep inc rnd every 3rd rnd 0 (1, 2, 3) times more—320 (352, 384, 416) sts.

Work even in pats until yoke measures 8½ (9, 9½,10)"/21.5 (23, 24, 25.5)cm from rnd 1 of yoke chart.

**For Sizes 3x and 4x Only**

**Inc rnd** [Work to increase marker, M1R, sm, k1, sm, M1L] 16 times, work to end—32 sts inc'd.

Cont in pats as established, rep inc rnd every 3rd rnd 3 times more—416 sts.

**Body only inc rnd** *[Work to increase marker, M1R, sm, k1, sm, M1L] 2 times, [work to increase marker, sm, k1, sm] 4 times, [work to increase marker, M1R, sm, k1, sm, M1L] 2 times; rep from * once more, work to end—16 sts inc'd.

Cont in pats as established, rep body only inc rnd every 3rd rnd 0 (1) time more—432 (448) sts.

Work even in pats until yoke measures 10½ (11)"/26.5 (28)cm from rnd 1 of yoke chart.

**Separate Body and Sleeves**

**Note** Remove shaping markers only on next rnd.

**Next rnd** Work in pat over 41 (45, 49, 53, 57, 61, 65) sts, place next 57 (65, 73, 81, 89, 89, 89) sts on st holder for sleeve, cast on 8 sts, work in pat over 87 (95, 103, 111, 119, 127, 135) sts

for front, place next 57 (65, 73, 81, 89, 89, 89) sts on holder for sleeve, cast on 8 sts, work in pat over rem 46 (50, 54, 58, 62, 66, 70) sts—190 (206, 222, 238, 254, 270, 286) sts for body. Work even in pats, working cable panels as established and rem sts in St st (k every rnd), for 2"/5cm.

**Waist Shaping**

**Inc rnd** *K to marker, sm, work cable panel chart over 5 sts, sm, k1, M1L, k to 1 st before next marker, M1R, k1, sm, work cable panel over 5 sts, sm; rep from * once more, k to end    4 sts inc'd.

Rep inc rnd every 12th rnd 6 times more—218 (234, 250, 266, 282, 298, 314) sts.

Work even in pats until piece measures 15¼"/38.5cm from underarm, end with a rnd 2 of cable panel.

**Next rnd** *K1, p1; rep from * around.

Rep last rnd for k1, p1 rib for 1¼"/3cm.

Knit 2 rnds.

Bind off.

**Sleeves**

Place 57 (65, 73, 81, 89, 89, 89) sts for sleeve onto larger dpn. Beg at center of underarm, pick up and k 4 sts, work 57 (65, 73, 81, 89, 89, 89) sts in pat, pick up and k 4 sts—65 (73, 81,

89, 97, 97, 97) sts. Pm for beg of rnd.
Work even in pat, working 5 sts in cable panel as established
and k rem sts, until sleeve measures 13"/33cm.
Change to smaller dpn.

For sizes Small, Medium, and Large only
**Dec rnd** [K2tog, p2tog] 7 (8, 9) times, k2tog, [p1, k1] twice, p1,
[k2tog, p2tog] 7 (8, 9) times, p1, k1—36 (40, 44) sts.

For sizes 1X, 2X, 3X, and 4X only
**Dec rnd** K2, *k2tog; rep from * to last st,
k1—46 (50, 50, 50) sts.
Work even in k1, p1 rib for 5"/12.5cm. Knit 2 rnds.
Bind off.

FINISHING
Weave in ends. Block to measurements. •

## YOKE CHART

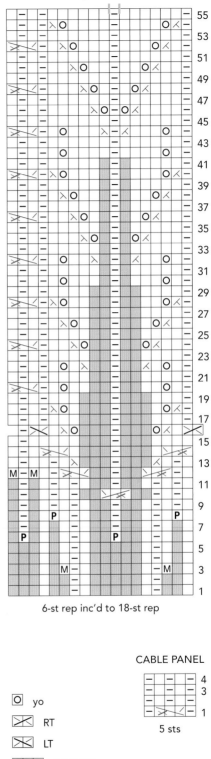

6-st rep inc'd to 18-st rep

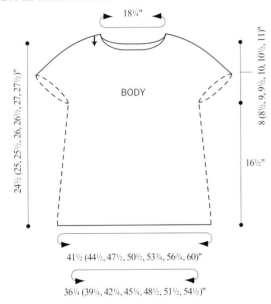

18¼"

BODY

24½ (25, 25½, 26, 26½, 27, 27½)"

8 (8½, 9, 9½, 10, 10½, 11)"

16½"

41½ (44½, 47½, 50½, 53¾, 56¾, 60)"

36¼ (39¼, 42¼, 45¼, 48½, 51½, 54½)"

↓ = Direction of work

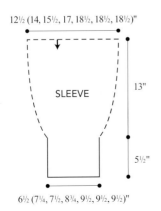

12½ (14, 15½, 17, 18½, 18½, 18½)"

SLEEVE

13"

5½"

6½ (7¼, 7½, 8¾, 9½, 9½, 9½)"

## STITCH KEY

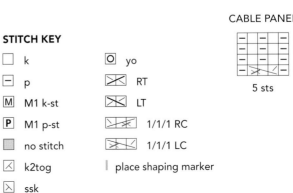

|  |  |
| --- | --- |
| ☐ | k |
| − | p |
| M | M1 k-st |
| P | M1 p-st |
| (shaded) | no stitch |
| ╱ | k2tog |
| ╲ | ssk |
| O | yo |
| ╳ | RT |
| ╳ | LT |
| ╱ | 1/1/1 RC |
| ╲ | 1/1/1 LC |
| ❘ | place shaping marker |

## CABLE PANEL

| | | | | 4 |
| | | | | 3 |
| | | | | 1 |

5 sts

# BELL SLEEVE PULLOVER

The unique silhouette of Laura Zukaite's delicate pullover comes courtesy of set-in bell sleeves and a gently scooped neck. The allover autumnal pattern hits all the right notes, and twisted rib provides the finishing at the lower hem, sleeve cuffs, and neckline.

■■■◻

## SIZES
Small (Medium/Large, 1X/2X, 3X).
Shown in size Small.

## KNITTED MEASUREMENTS
**Bust** 36 (46, 55, 63½)"/91.5 (117, 139.5, 161)cm
**Length** 23½ (24½, 25½, 26½)"/59.5 (62, 64.5, 67.5)cm
**Upper arm** 14 (14, 16¼, 16¼)"/35.5 (35.5, 41, 41)cm

## MATERIALS
• 5 (6, 7, 8) 3½oz/100g hanks (each approx 220yd/200m) of **Ancient Arts Fibre Crafts** Lascaux Worsted (punta arenas wool/manx loaghtan wool) in Petal (**4**)
• One size 8 (5mm) circular needle, 32"/80cm long, OR SIZE TO OBTAIN GAUGES
• One size 7 (4.5mm) circular needle, 24"/60cm long
• Stitch markers
• Stitch holders

## GAUGE
• 18 sts and 22 rows to 4"/10cm over St st using larger needle.
• 18 sts and 26 rows to 4"/10cm over lace chart using larger needle.
TAKE TIME TO CHECK GAUGES.

## NOTE
**1)** Slip the first st and knit the last st of every row.
**2)** When shaping into lace pats, only work a decrease if there are corresponding yarnover(s), and vice versa.
**3)** Circular needle is used to accommodate the large number of sts. Do not join.

## STITCH GLOSSARY
**S3K2P** Sl 3 sts tog, k2tog, then pass 3 slipped sts over the k2tog—4 sts dec'd.

## BACK
With larger needles, cast on 83 (103, 123, 143) sts.
**Row 1 (WS)** Sl 1, *k1, p1 tbl; rep from * to last 2 sts, k2.
**Row 2 (RS)** Sl 1, *p1, k1 tbl; rep from * to last 2 sts, p1, k1.
Rep last 2 rows for twisted rib for 1"/2.5cm, end with a WS row.

### Begin Chart
**Row 1 (RS)** Sl 1, work 20-st rep 4 (5, 6, 7) times, work last st of chart, k1.
**Row 2** Sl 1, work chart as established to last st, k1.
Cont to work chart in this way until piece measures 16"/40.5cm from beg, end with a WS row.

### Armhole Shaping
**Next row (RS)** Bind off 3 (6, 8, 10) sts, work to end.
**Next row** Bind off 3 (6, 8, 10) sts, work to last 2 sts, k2tog.
**Next 0 (2, 2, 2) rows** Bind off 0 (4, 5, 7) sts, work to last 2 sts, k2tog.
**Next 2 (2, 4, 8) rows** Bind off 2 sts, work to last 2 sts, k2tog.
**Next 2 (2, 2, 0) rows** Bind off 1 st, work to the last 2 sts, k2tog.
**Next row** Work to last 2 sts, k2tog—65 (69, 77, 81) sts.
Work even in pat until armhole measures 7½ (8½, 9½, 10½)"/19 (21.5, 24, 26.5)cm, end with a RS row.
**Next row (WS)** Work 17 (18, 20, 21) sts in pat, place on st holder for shoulder, bind off center 31 (33, 37, 39) sts, work rem 17 (18, 20, 21) sts in pat and place on st holder for shoulder.

## FRONT
Work as for back through armhole shaping, then work even until the armhole measures 2¾ (3¾, 4¾, 5¾)"/7 (9.5, 12, 14.5)cm, end with a WS row—65 (69, 77, 81) sts.

## Neck Shaping

**Next row (RS)** Work 27 (28, 30, 31) sts in pat, bind off center 11 (13, 17, 19) sts, work to end in pat.

**Next row** Work in pat to last 2 sts of first side, work 2 tog in pat; bind off 1 st at beg of 2nd side, work to end—1 st dec'd each side.

Working both sides at once, rep last row 9 times more—17 (18, 20, 21) sts rem each side.

Work even in pat until armhole measures 7½ (8½, 9½, 10½)"/ 19 (21.5, 24, 26.5)cm, end with a WS row. Place sts each side on st holders.

## SLEEVES

With larger needles, cast on 43 sts. Work in twisted rib as for back for 1"/2.5cm, end with a RS row.

**Inc row (WS)** Sl 1, k1, *pfb, kfb; rep from * to last st, k1—83 sts.

## Begin Chart

**Row 1 (RS)** Sl 1, work 20-st rep 4 times, work last st of chart, k1.

**Row 2** Sl 1, work chart as established to last st, k1.

Cont to work chart as established through row 30.

**Dec row (RS)** Sl 1, p2tog, work row 1 as established to last 3 sts, p2tog, k1—2 sts dec'd.

Rep dec row every other (other, 4th, 4th) row 9 (9, 4, 4) times more—63 (63, 73, 73) sts.

Cont in chart as established until piece measures 16 (16½, 17, 18)"/40.5 (42, 43, 45.5)cm from beg, end with a WS row.

## Cap shaping

**Next row (RS)** Bind off 3 (6, 8, 10) sts, work to end.

**Next row** Bind off 3 (6, 8, 10) sts, work to last 2 sts, k2tog.

**Next 2 rows** Bind off 2 (4, 5, 7) sts, work to last 2 sts, k2tog.

**Next 2 rows** Bind off 1 st, work to the last 2 sts, k2tog.

**Next row** Work to last 2 sts, k2tog—45 (35, 39, 31) sts.

Work even in pat for 7 (13, 13, 23) rows, end with a WS row.

**Dec row (RS)** Bind off 1 st, work to last 2 sts, k2tog—2 sts dec'd.

Rep dec row every 4th (4th, 4th, 6th) row 2 (7, 8, 5) times, then every other row 10 (0, 1, 0) times—19 sts.

Work 1 WS row. Bind off.

## FINISHING

Block pieces to measurements. Join shoulder seams using 3-needle bind-off (see page 164). Set in sleeves. Sew sleeve and side seams.

## Neckband

With RS facing, smaller needle, beg at left shoulder seam, pick up and k 90 (94, 102, 106) sts evenly around neck edge. Join and pm for beg of rnd.

**Rnd 1** *K1 tbl, p1; rep from * around.

Rep rnd 1 for twisted rib for 1½"/4cm. Bind off knitwise. Weave in ends.•

## STITCH KEY

| | |
|---|---|
| ☐ | k on RS, p on WS |
| ⊟ | p on RS, k on WS |
| ◯ | yo |
| ℺ | k1 tbl |
| ▨ | no stitch |
| ⟋ | k2tog |
| ⟍ | ssk |
| ⼈ | S2KP |
| ⟍ | sssk |
| ⼈ | k3tog |
| ⼈ | S3K2P |

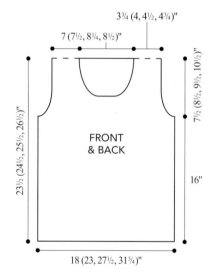

FRONT & BACK

3¾ (4, 4½, 4¾)"
7 (7½, 8¼, 8½)"
7½ (8½, 9½, 10½)"
23½ (24½, 25½, 26½)"
16"
18 (23, 27½, 31¾)"

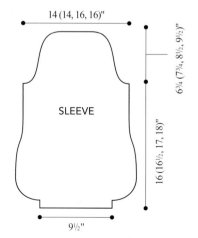

SLEEVE

14 (14, 16, 16)"
6¾ (7¾, 8½, 9½)"
16 (16½, 17, 18)"
9½"

# DIAMOND ARCHWAYS SCARF

Stylish, sophisticated, and at the ready to dress up or down, Amy Gunderson's versatile scarf is light as air with a narrow panel of zigzag lace running alongside a wider swath of diamonds. Show off these luxe stitches draped across your shoulders or doubled up for a cozier feel.

### KNITTED MEASUREMENTS
**Width** 22"/56cm
**Length** 64"/162.5cm

### MATERIALS
• 2 1¾oz/50g skeins (each approx 440yd/400m) of **Fibra Natura/Universal Yarn** Whisper Lace (superwash wool/silk) in #104 Fog ( **1** )
• One pair size 4 (3.5mm) needles, OR SIZE TO OBTAIN GAUGE
• Stitch markers

### GAUGE
21 sts and 24 rows to 4"/10cm over lace pats using size 4 (3.5mm) needles.
TAKE TIME TO CHECK GAUGE.

### NOTE
Slip the first stitch of every row purlwise wyif for selvage st.

SCARF
Cast on 120 sts.
**Row 1 (RS)** Sl 1, k to end.
Rep last row for garter st for 7 rows more.
**Next row (WS)** Sl 1, k4, pm, p37, pm, p73, pm, k5.

JACK DEUTSCH

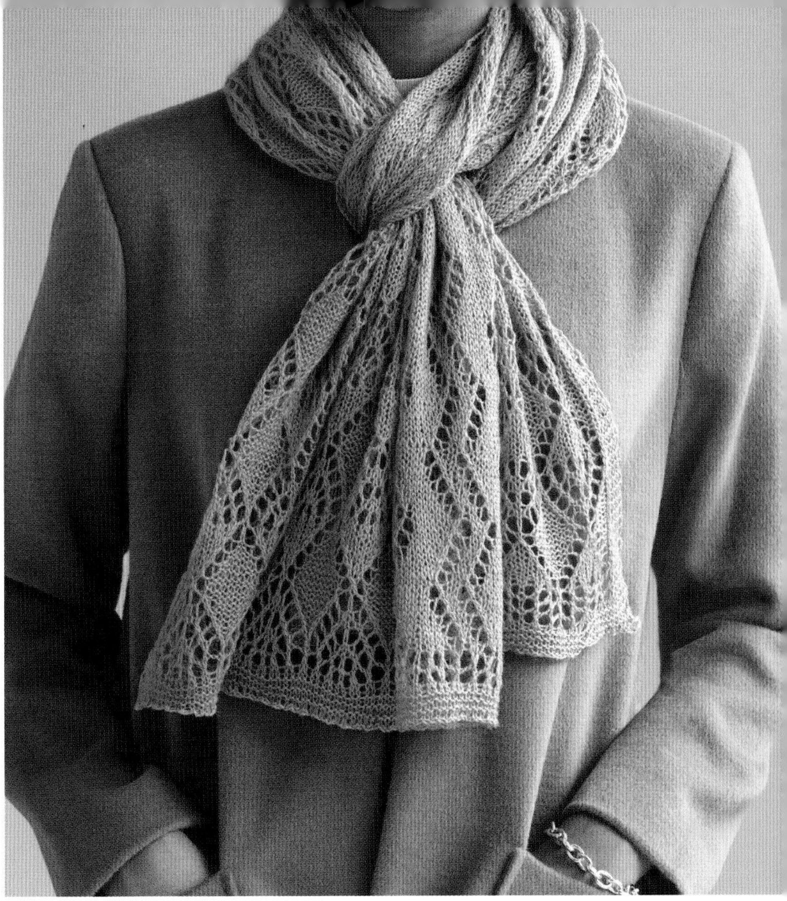

Begin Lower Edge Lace Pattern

**Row 1 (RS)** Sl 1, k to marker, sm, [k2tog, yo] 3 times, *k1, [yo, ssk] twice, yo, SK2P, yo, [k2tog, yo] twice*, rep between *s 4 times more, k1, [yo, ssk] 3 times, sm, rep between *s 3 times, k1, sm, k to end.

**Row 2 (WS)** Sl 1, k to marker, sm, p to last marker, sm, k5.

Rep rows 1 and 2 once more for lower edge lace pat.

Begin Charts

**Row 1 (RS)** Sl 1, k to marker; work row 1 of chart 1 to marker as foll: work first 6 sts of chart, work 12-st rep 5 times, work last 7 sts of chart; sm, work row 1 of chart 2 to marker as foll: work 12-st rep 3 times, work last st of chart; k to end.

Cont in pats as established until 20 rows of charts have been worked 20 times.

Begin Top Edge Lace Pattern

Work 4 rows as for lower edge lace pat.

Knit 8 rows. Bind off all sts.

FINISHING

Weave in ends. Run blocking wires along all sides of piece. Stretch wires and pin to blocking boards to open up lace. Block to measurements.•

CHART 1

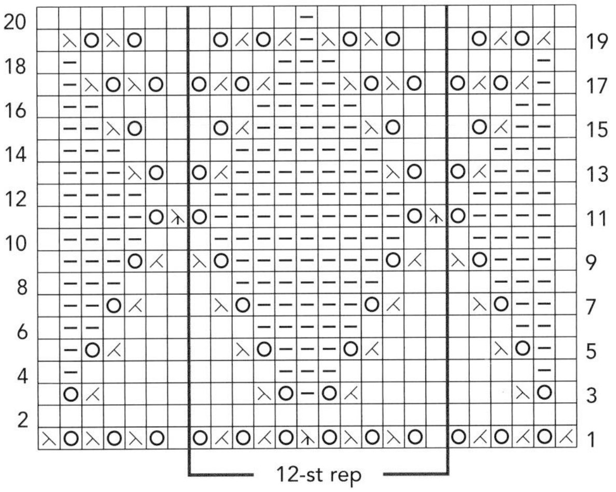


CHART 2

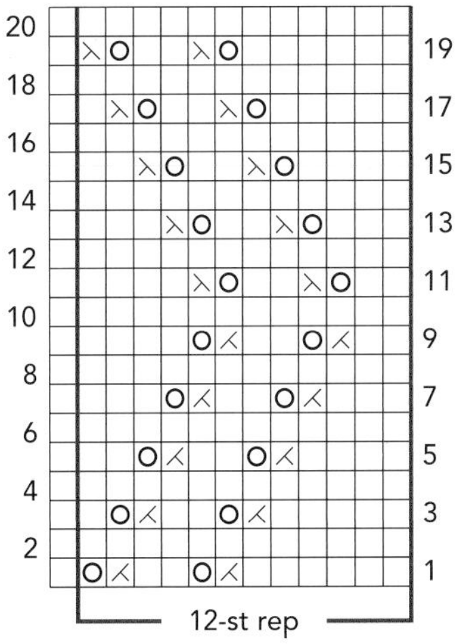


**STITCH KEY**

| | | | | | |
|---|---|---|---|---|---|
| □ | k on RS, p on WS | ⟋ | k2tog | ⋏ | SK2P |
| ⊟ | p on RS, k on WS | ⟍ | ssk | ○ | yo |

# WINTER LAKE STOLE

If you're in the market for a show-stopping statement piece, Caroline Sommerfeld has ingeniously combined multiple patterns into a long stole that fits the bill. Inspired by a sunrise over a prairie lake in winter, slip-stitch rib, an undulating wave pattern, Bargello slip-stitch fade, and a slip-stitch fade band play out like paints across a canvas.

### KNITTED MEASUREMENTS
Approx 20 ½ x 77"/52 x 195.5cm

### MATERIALS
• 1  3½oz/100g hank (each approx 263yd/240m) of **Ancient Arts Fibre Crafts** Nettle Soft DK (merino wool/nettle) each in Antique (A), Grannies in Lace (B), Bien! (C), and Paperweight (D) (3)
• One size 7 (4.5mm) circular needle, 24"/60cm long, OR SIZE TO OBTAIN GAUGES
• Stitch markers

### GAUGES
• 17 sts and 23 rows to 4"/10cm over St st using size 7 (4.5mm) needle.
• 18 sts and 20 rows to 4"/10cm over undulating waves pat using size 7 (4.5mm) needle.
TAKE TIME TO CHECK GAUGES.

### NOTE
Circular needle is used to accommodate the large number of sts. Do not join.

### STOLE
With A, cast on using I-cord cast-on as foll: cast on 3 sts, *sl 3 sts back to LH needle, kfb, k2; rep from * until there are 95 sts on needle.

### Begin Undulating Waves Chart
**Row 1 (RS)** Work to rep line, work 11-st rep 8 times, work to end of chart.
Cont to work chart as established until rows 1–28 have been worked 3 times.

### Begin Slip-Stitch Rib Pattern
**Set-up row 1 (RS)** Sl 1 wyib, sl 1 wyif, k to last 3 sts, k1, sl 1 wyif, p1.
**Set-up row 2** Sl 1 wyib, k1, sl 1 wyif, p to last 3 sts, sl 1 wyif, k1, p1.
**Row 1 (RS)** Sl 1 wyib, sl 1 wyif, k to last 3 sts, k1, sl 1 wyif, p1.
**Row 2** Sl 1 wyib, k1, sl 1 wyif, *k1, p1; rep from * to last 4 sts, k1, sl 1 wyif, k1, p1.
**Row 3** Sl 1 wyib, sl 1 wyif, k1, *sl 1 wyib, k1; rep from * to last 4 sts, sl 1 wyib, k1, sl 1 wyif, p1.
**Row 4** Rep row 2.
With A, rep rows 1 and 2.
With B, rep rows 3 and 4.
Rep last 4 rows twice more.
With B, rep rows 1–4.

### Begin Undulating Waves Chart
With B, work rows 1–28 of undulating waves chart 3 times as before.

### Begin Bargello Slip-Stitch Fade Chart
**Row 1 (RS)** With B, work to rep line, work 4-st rep 22 times, work to end of chart.
Cont to work chart as established, changing to C as indicated on chart, until rows 1–8 have been worked 4 times.

### Begin Undulating Waves Chart
With C, work rows 1–28 of undulating waves chart 3 times as before.

## UNDULATING WAVES

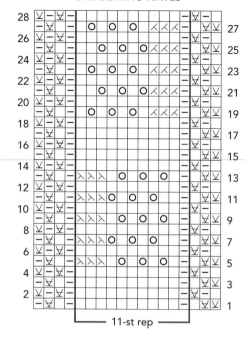

11-st rep

## SLIP-STITCH FADE

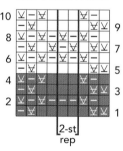

2-st rep

## BARGELLO
## SLIP-STITCH FADE

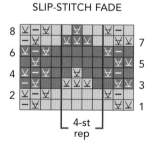

4-st rep

**Begin Slip-Stitch Fade Chart**

**Row 1 (RS)** With C, work to rep line, work 2-st rep 44 times, work to end of chart.

Cont to work chart as established, changing to D as indicated on chart, until rows 1–10 have been worked 3 times, then work rows 1 and 2 once more.

**Begin Undulating Waves Chart**

With D, work rows 1–28 of undulating waves chart 3 times as before, then work rows 1–4 once more.

With D, bind off using I-cord bind-off as foll: *k2, k2tog tbl, sl 3 sts back to LH needle, rep from * until all sts are bound off.

**FINISHING**

Weave in ends. Block to measurements.•

## STITCH & COLOR KEY

| | | | |
|---|---|---|---|
| ☐ | k on RS, p on WS | ▨ | A |
| ⊟ | p on RS, k on WS | ▨ | B |
| ⊿ | k2tog | ▨ | C |
| ⊠ | ssk | ☐ | D |
| ⊙ | yo | | |
| ⊻ | sl 1 wyif | | |
| ⊻ | sl 1 wyib | | |

# LACE COCOON CARDI

Joan McGowan-Michael's lacy bell-sleeve cocoon cardigan is knit in three pieces for one altogether dramatic look. The two body pieces are worked in a Frost Flowers pattern with their ribbed edges before joining at the back. The lower border is picked up along one edge and worked downward in a mesh stitch that finishes with a simple rib.

### SIZES
Small (Medium/Large, X-Large/1X).
Shown in size Medium/Large.

### KNITTED MEASUREMENTS
**Center back length** 33"/84cm
**Center back to cuff length** 27 (29, 31)"/68.5 (73.5, 78.5)cm

### MATERIALS
• 12 (13, 14)  1¾oz/50g balls (each approx 98yd/89m) of **Stacy Charles Fine Yarns/ Tahki•Stacy Charles** Patti (cotton) in #02 Rose Quartz (4)
• One pair size 9 (5.5mm) needles, OR SIZE TO OBTAIN GAUGE
• Removable stitch markers

### GAUGE
17 sts and 22 rows to 4"/10cm over chart, after blocking, using size 9 (5.5mm) needles.
TAKE TIME TO CHECK GAUGE.

## CARDI
### Right Front Panel
Beg at cuff edge, cast on 120 sts.
**Row 1 (RS)** *K1, p1; rep from * to end.
Rep this row for k1, p1 rib for 1½"/4cm.

Begin chart
**Row 1 (RS)** [K1, p1] 8 times (for 16-st rib band), pm, work first st of chart, work 34-st rep 3 times, work last st of chart.

**Row 2 (WS)** Work row 2 of chart over 104 sts, sm, rib 16. Cont to foll chart and rib band pat as established until there are 132 (144, 156) rows worked in the chart, ending with chart row 12 (24, 12). Piece measures approx 25½ (27½, 29½)"/65 (70, 75)cm from beg. Bind off.

### Left Front Panel
Cast on and work the rib edge as for the right front panel.

### Begin chart
**Row 1 (RS)** Work first st of chart, work 34-st rep 3 times, work last st of chart, pm, [p1, k1] 8 times (for 16-st rib band).
**Row 2** Rib 16, work row 2 of chart pat over 104 sts.
Cont to foll chart and rib band pat as established, until there are same number of rows as right front panel. Bind off.

### FINISHING
Seam panels tog along bound-off edges for center back seam.

### Lower Border
Place removable st markers at 9"/23cm from cast-on edge of each front panel. With RS facing, pick up and k 137 (152, 167) sts between markers.
**Row 1 (WS)** Purl.
**Row 2 (RS)** K3, *k2tog, yo, k1; rep from * to last 2 sts, k2.
**Row 3** Purl.
**Row 4** K3, *yo, k1, k2tog; rep from * to last 2 sts, k2.
Rep rows 1–4 until lower border measures 7½"/19cm. Then, work in k1, p1 rib for 1½"/4cm more. Bind off.

### Sleeve Cuffs
Place markers at 2¾"/7cm above bound-off edge of lower border and 2¾"/7cm above cast-on edges of each front panel. Work each side as foll:
With RS facing, pick up and k 52 sts between these newly placed markers.
Work in k1, p1 rib for 1½"/4cm. Bind off in rib.
Seam the sleeve cuffs and the rem 2¾"/7cm seam left open to close the lower edge.

Weave in ends. Block lightly to measurements.•

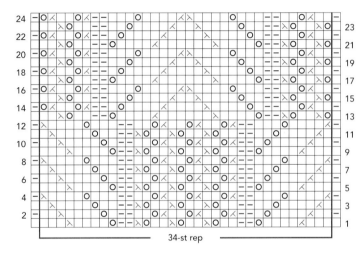

34-st rep

### STITCH KEY

☐ k on RS, p on WS

▭ p on RS, k on WS

⟋ k2tog on RS, p2tog on WS

⟍ ssk on RS, p2tog tbl on WS

Ⓞ yo

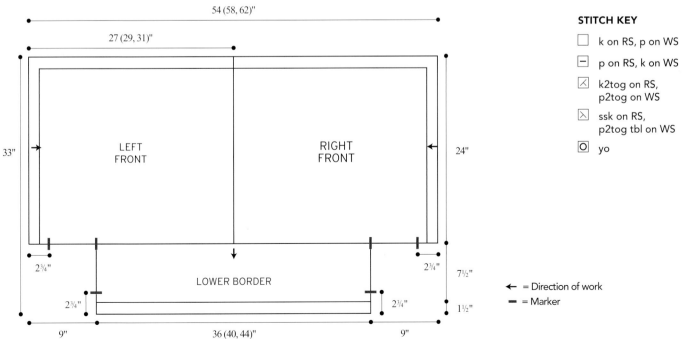

← = Direction of work

▬ = Marker

# WRAPAROUND V-NECK

Joan Forgione takes a relaxed-fit, V-neck pullover and kicks it up a notch with an eye-catching four-row lace pattern that wraps around into the stockinette front. Beginning with a provisional cast-on, the sweater is knit top-down, with sleeves knit separately and sewn to the body in finishing.

## SIZES
Small (Medium, Large, X-Large).
Shown in size Small.

## KNITTED MEASUREMENTS
**Bust** 39 (42, 47, 51)"/99 (106.5, 119, 129.5)cm
**Length** 19 ½ (20 ½, 21 ½, 22 ½)"/49.5 (52, 54.5, 57)cm
**Upper arm** 11 ½ (12 ¼, 13 ½, 14 ½)"/29 (31, 34, 37)cm

## MATERIALS
• 8 (9, 11, 12) 1¾oz/50g balls (each approx 137yd/125m) of **Rowan** Cotton Cashmere (cotton/cashmere) in #211 Linen (4)
• One each sizes 5 and 7 (3.75 and 4.5mm) circular needle, each 32"/80cm long, OR SIZE TO OBTAIN GAUGES
• One size 5 (3.75mm) circular needle, 16"/40cm long
• One extra size 7 (4.5mm) needle
• One set (5) each sizes 5 and 7 (3.75 and 4.5mm) double-pointed needles (dpn)
• One size 7 (4.5mm) crochet hook
• Stitch holders
• Stitch markers
• Scrap yarn for provisional cast-on

## GAUGES
• 19 sts and 29 rows/rnds to 4"/10cm over St st using larger needle.
• 17 sts and 28 rows/rnds to 4"/10cm over lace pat st using larger needle.
TAKE TIME TO CHECK GAUGES.

## PROVISIONAL CAST-ON
Using scrap yarn and crochet hook, ch the number of sts to cast on plus a few extra. Cut a tail and pull tail through last chain. With knitting needle and yarn, pick up and knit stated number of sts through "purl bumps" on back of chain. To remove scrap yarn chain, when instructed, pull out tail from last crochet stitch. Gently and slowly pull on tail to unravel crochet stitches, carefully placing each released knit stitch on a needle.

## STITCH GLOSSARY
**M1R** Insert LH needle from back to front under the strand between last st worked and next st on LH needle. K into the front loop to twist the st.
**M1L** Insert LH needle from front to back under the strand between last st worked and next st on LH needle. K into the back loop to twist the st.

## LACE PATTERN STITCH
(worked in rows over a multiple of 4 sts plus 1)
**Row 1 (RS)** *P1, k3; rep from * to last st, p1.
**Row 2** *K1, p3; rep from * to last st, k1.
**Row 3** *P1, yo, SK2P, yo; rep from * to last st, p1.
**Row 4** *K1, p3; rep from * to last st, k1.
Rep rows 1–4 for lace pat st worked in rows.

## LACE PATTERN STITCH
(worked in rnds over a multiple of 4 sts)
**Rnds 1 and 2** *P1, k3; rep from * around.
**Rnd 3** *P1, yo, SK2P, yo; rep from * around.
**Rnd 4** *P1, k3; rep from * around.
Rep rnds 1–4 for lace pat st worked in rnds.

## NOTE
The pullover is worked from the shoulders down to the lower hem edge, first in rows back and forth, and separately to the end of the armholes, then in one piece in rounds to the lower edge. The sleeves are worked in rounds on dpn from cuff edge to upper arm and then seamed to body at the armhole openings.

## FRONT

### Left Shoulder

With crochet hook and scrap yarn, using the provisional cast-on method, cast on 31 (35, 39, 43) sts. Then, with larger needles and working yarn, work in St st (k on RS, p on WS) for 6 rows.

**Neck inc row (RS)** K2, M1R, k to end.

Rep neck inc row every other row 15 (15, 17, 17) times more—47 (51, 57, 61) sts.

Purl 1 row. Place sts on st holder.

### Right Shoulder

With crochet hook and scrap yarn, using the provisional cast-on method, cast on 31 (35, 39, 43) sts. Then, with larger needles and working yarn, work in St st for 6 rows.

**Neck inc row (RS)** K to last 2 sts, M1L, k2.

Rep neck inc row every other row 15 (15, 17, 17) times more—47 (51, 57, 61) sts.

Purl 1 row.

### Join Shoulders

**Next row (RS)** K47 (51, 57, 61) sts from right shoulder, k1 from left shoulder, M1, k to end of left shoulder—95 (103, 115, 123) sts.

Work even in St st until armhole edge measures 6 (6½, 7, 7½)"/15 (16.5, 18, 19)cm. Leave sts on hold for front to be worked later with the back.

## BACK

Carefully take out provisional cast-on for 31 (35, 39, 43) sts for right shoulder and place these sts on larger needle and work first RS row as foll: p1, k3, p2tog, *k3, p1; rep from * to last 9 sts, k3, p2tog, k3, p1—29 (33, 37, 41) sts.

Then, beg with row 2, work in lace pat for 7 rows more. Leave sts on hold.

Work left shoulder sts in same way.

### Join at Neck Edge

**Next row (RS)** Work left shoulder sts, cast on 27 (27, 31, 31) sts, work right shoulder sts—85 (93, 105, 113) sts.

Work even in lace pat st in rows until armhole edge measures 6 (6½, 7, 7½)"/15 (16.5, 18, 19)cm.

## BODY

**Next rnd** Work back sts in lace pat as established, pm, k front sts, pm to mark beg of rnd and join to work in rnds—180 (196, 220, 236) sts.

**Next 2 rnds** Work in lace pat in rnds as established to marker, sm, k to end of rnd.

**Note** At this point, the sts in lace pat will be inc'd while, at the same time, the sts in St st will be dec'd so overall st count remains the same.

**Note** When working in lace pat, only work a yo before and after the SK2P when there are a sufficient number of sts to work this lace detail. Otherwise, work as k only or as a single yo and SKP (or SKP, yo at the inside of this pat) until there are a sufficient number of sts for the rep.

**Displacement rnd** M1R, work in lace pat to marker, M1L, sm, k2, ssk, k to 4 sts before last marker, k2tog, k2.

Rep displacement rnd every 3rd rnd, incorporating inc'd sts into lace pat, 29 (31, 33, 35) times more, end with lace pat rnd 4. There will be 35 (39, 47, 51) sts in St st and 145 (157, 173, 185) sts in lace pat and piece will measure approx 18½ (19½, 20½, 21½)"/47 (49.5, 52, 54.5)cm from shoulder on back or front. Change to smaller needle.

**Next inc rnd** *P1, work (k1, p1, k1) into next st, [p1, k1] 5 times; rep from * to 13 (13, 17, 17) sts before marker, then [p1, k1] 0 (0, 2, 2) times, p1, (k1, p1, k1) into next st, [p1, k1] 4 times, p1, (k1, p1, k1) into next st, p1, sm, **k1, p1; rep from ** to last st, k1—206 (224, 250, 268) sts.

Cont in k1, p1 rib for 1"/2.5cm more.

Bind off in rib.

## SLEEVES

Beg at cuff edge with smaller dpn, cast on 46 (50, 54, 58) sts.

Divide sts over 4 dpn and join to work in rnds.

Work in rnds of k1, p1 rib for 1"/2.5cm.

Change to larger dpn.

Work in St st (k every rnd) for 2 rnds.

**Inc rnd** K2, M1L, k to last 2 sts of rnd, M1R, k2—2 sts inc'd.

Rep inc rnd every 27 rnds for 3 (3, 4, 4) times more—54 (58, 64, 68) sts.

Work even until piece measures 16 (16½, 17, 17)"/40.5 (42, 43, 43)cm from beg. Bind off.

## FINISHING

Sew sleeves into armhole openings.

### Neckband

With RS facing and using smaller, shorter circular needle, pick up and k 40 (40, 44, 44) sts from back neck edge, 30 (30, 34, 34) sts from left side of V-neck, pm, 1 st in the center of V-neck, 30 (30, 34, 34) sts from right side of V-neck—101 (101, 113, 113) sts. Join to work in rnds and pm to mark beg of rnds.

**Rnd 1** *P1, k1; rep from * to 1 st before center V-neck marker, place new marker, S2KP and remove previous marker, then **k1, p1; rep from ** to end.

**Rnd 2** Work even in rib.

**Rnds 3–6** Rep rnds 1 and 2 twice more.

Bind off in rib.

Weave in ends. Block finished piece lightly to measurements.•

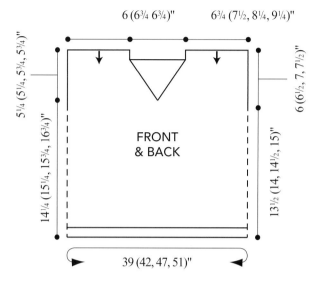

6 (6¾ 6¾)"        6¾ (7½, 8¼, 9¼)"

5¼ (5¼, 5¾, 5¾)"

14¼ (15¼, 15¾, 16¾)"

FRONT & BACK

13½ (14, 14½, 15)"

6 (6½, 7, 7½)"

39 (42, 47, 51)"

↓ = Direction of work

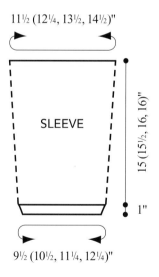

11½ (12¼, 13½, 14½)"

SLEEVE

15 (15½, 16, 16)"

1"

9½ (10½, 11¼, 12¼)"

# GARTER AND LACE SHAWL

The perfect complement to any understated outfit, Julie Turjoman's asymmetrical shawl is worked on the diagonal and features two subtly different lace patterns of chevron and garter ridge, interspersed with sections of garter stitch, for lovely texture and visual interplay.

## KNITTED MEASUREMENTS
**Width** 64"/162.5cm
**Length** 48"/122cm

## MATERIALS
• 1 3½oz/100g hanks (each approx 439yd/400m) of **Valley Yarns** Charlemont (wool/silk/polyamide) in #10 Whipple Blue (1)
• One size 6 (4mm) circular needle, 32"/80cm long, OR SIZE TO OBTAIN GAUGE
• Stitch markers

## GAUGE
• 24 sts and 44 rows to 4"/10cm over garter st using size 6 (4mm) needles.
TAKE TIME TO CHECK GAUGE.

## NOTE
Circular needle is used to accommodate the large number of sts. Do not join.

### SHAWL
Cast on 1 st.
**Next row** Kfb.
**Next row** Kfb, k1—3 sts.

### Begin Garter Section
**Garter row 1 (RS)** K to last st, kfb—1 st inc'd.
**Garter row 2** Kfb, k to end—1 st inc'd.
**Garter row 3** K1, k2tog, k to last st, kfb.
**Garter row 4** Kfb, k to end—1 st inc'd.
Rep garter rows 1–4 until there are 72 sts.

### Begin Garter Ridge Lace Chart
**Note** Work an additional 10-st rep of chart pat after 10 sts have been inc'd at end of RS rows, moving end of row marker to end of last rep.
**Row 1 (RS)** K1, pm, *k1, yo, k3, SK2P, k3, yo; rep from * to last st, pm, kfb—1 st inc'd.
**Row 2** Kfb, k to marker, sm, p to marker, sm, k1—1 st inc'd.
**Row 3** K1, sm, *k2, yo, k2, SK2P, k2, yo, k1; rep from * to marker, sm, k to last st, k1.
**Row 4** Rep row 2.
**Row 5** K1, sm, *k3, yo, k1, SK2P, k1, yo, k2; rep from * to marker, sm, k to last st, kfb—1 st inc'd.
**Row 6** Rep row 2.
**Row 7** K1, sm, *k4, yo, SK2P, yo, k3; rep from * to marker, sm, k to last st, k1.
**Row 8** Rep row 2.
**Row 9** Purl.
**Row 10** Knit.
Rep rows 1–10 twice more—90 sts.

**Rep garter rows 1–4 three times more**—99 sts.

### Begin Chevron Lace Chart
**Note** Work an additional 10-st rep of chart pat after 10 sts have been inc'd at end of RS rows, moving end of row marker to end of last rep.
**Row 1 (RS)** K1, sm, *k1, yo, k3, S2KP, k3, yo; rep from * to marker, sm, k to last st, kfb—1 st inc'd.

**Row 2** Kfb, k to marker, sm, *p9, k1; rep from * to last st, sm, k1—1 st inc'd.
**Row 3** K1, sm, *p2, yo, k2, S2KP, k2, yo, p1; rep from * to marker, sm, k to end.
**Row 4** Kfb, k to marker, sm, *k1, p7, k2; rep from * to last st, sm, k1—1 st inc'd.
**Row 5** K1, sm, *p3, yo, k1, S2KP, k1, yo, p2; rep from * to marker, sm, k to last st, kfb—1 st inc'd.
**Row 6** Kfb, k to marker, sm, *k2, p5, k3; rep from * to last st, sm, k1—1 st inc'd.
**Row 7** K1, sm, *p4, yo, S2KP, yo, p3; rep from * to marker, sm, k to end.
**Row 8** Kfb, k to marker, sm, p to marker, sm, k1—1 st inc'd.
Rep rows 1–8 twice more—117 sts.

Rep between **s (12 garter rows with inc) once—126 sts.
Beg with 1 st before chart marker at beg of row and 5 sts after last chart marker at end and working inc as before, rep rows 1–10 of garter ridge lace chart 3 times—144 sts.
Rep between **s (12 garter rows with inc) once—153 sts.
Beg with 1 st before chart marker at beg of row and 2 sts after last chart marker at end and working inc as before, rep rows 1–8 of chevron lace chart 3 times—171 sts.
Rep between **s (12 garter rows with inc) once—180 sts.
Bind off loosely on RS.

FINISHING
Weave in ends. Block to measurements.•

GARTER RIDGE LACE

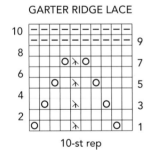

10-st rep

CHEVRON LACE

10-st rep

**STITCH KEY**

☐ k on RS, p on WS

⊟ p on RS, k on WS

O yo

⅄ SK2P

⅄ S2KP

# LACE AFLUTTER RUANA

Yoko Hatta's elegant light ruana will have you dreaming of beachy days and summer evenings. The piece is made up of two long rectangles knit from the lower front to lower back edges, each featuring a classic leaf pattern offset by k1, p1 ribbing at the sides and lower hem. The only finishing required is a center-back seam.

## KNITTED MEASUREMENTS
**Width (across back)** 36"/91.5cm
**Length (from shoulder)** 33½"/85cm*
*Due to the fiber content of this yarn, the knitted fabric has a tendency to stretch lengthwise while wearing.

## MATERIALS
• Original Yarn
12 1¾oz/50g balls (each approx 155yd/142m) of **Classic Elite Yarns** Firefly (viscose/linen) in #7719 Padua (3)
• Substitute Yarn
15 1¾oz/50g balls (each approx 131yd/118m) of **Lana Grossa/Linea Pura** Solo Lino (viscose/linen) in #39 Antique Violet (3)
• One pair size 6 (4mm) needles, or size to obtain gauge

## GAUGE
18 sts and 26 rows to 4"/10cm over lace pat using size 6 (4mm) needles.
TAKE TIME TO CHECK GAUGE.

## NOTE
Lace pattern may be worked from written instructions or chart.

## STITCH GLOSSARY
**sl 1, k2, psso** Sl 1 wyib, k2, pass sl st over k2 and off RH needle—1 st dec'd. (On foll row, a yo is worked to inc 1 st.)

## LACE PATTERN
(multiple of 16 sts plus 13)
**Row 1 (RS)** *P2, k4, p1, k4, p2, k3; rep from * to last 13 sts, p2, k4, p1, k4, p2.
**Row 2** K the knit sts and p the purl sts and yo's.

ROSE CALLAHAN

**Row 3** *P2, k1, k2tog, yo, k1, p1, k1, yo, ssk, k1, p2, sl 1, k2, psso; rep from *, end last rep p2.

**Row 4** K2, p4, k1, p4, k2, *p1, yo, p1, k2, p4, k1, p4, k2; rep from * to end.

**Row 5** *P2, k2tog, yo, k2, p1, k2, yo, ssk, p2, k3; rep from *, end last rep p2.

**Row 6** K the knit sts and p the purl sts and yo's.

**Row 7** *P2, k1, yo, k1, k2tog, p1, ssk, k1, yo, k1, p2, sl 1, k2, psso; rep from *, end last rep p2.

**Row 8** Rep row 4.

**Row 9** *P2, k1, yo, k1, k2tog, p1, ssk, k1, yo, k1, p2, k3; rep from *, end last rep p2.

**Row 10** K the knit sts and p the purl sts and yo's.

**Row 11** *P2, k2, k2tog, yo, p1, yo, ssk, k2, p2, sl 1, k2, psso; rep from *, end last rep p2.

**Row 12** Rep row 4.

**Row 13** *P2, k1, k2tog, yo, k1, p1, k1, yo, ssk, k1, p2, k3; rep from *, end last rep p2.

**Row 14** K the knit sts and p the purl sts and yo's.

**Row 15** *P2, k2tog, yo, k2, p1, k2, yo, ssk, p2, sl 1, k2, psso; rep from *, end last rep p2.

**Row 16** Rep row 4.

**Rows 17 and 18** Rep rows 9 and 10.

**Rows 19 and 20** Rep rows 7 and 8.

**Row 21** *P2, k2, k2tog, yo, p1, yo, ssk, k2, p2, k3; rep from *, end last rep p2.

**Row 22** K the knit sts and p the purl sts and yo's.

Rep rows 3–22 for lace pat.

LEFT FRONT AND 1/2 BACK
Cast on 89 sts.

**Row 1 (RS)** P1, *k1, p1; rep from * to end.

**Rows 2–4** K the knit sts and p the purl sts for k1, p1 rib.

Begin Lace Pattern

**Row 1 (RS)** [P1, k1] 3 times to cont rib, pm, work lace pat to last 6 sts, pm, [k1, p1] 3 times to cont rib.

Cont in pats as established, keeping first and last 6 sts in k1, p1 rib and rem sts in lace pat through pat row 22, then rep rows 3–22 of pat 21 times more.

Work in k1, p1 rib over all sts for 4 rows.

Bind off in rib.

RIGHT FRONT AND 1/2 BACK
Work same as left front and 1/2 back.

FINISHING
Weave in ends. Block pieces to measurements.

Lay both pieces next to each other, aligning bound-off edges. Beg at bound-off edges, sew two sides tog at center back for approx 30"/76cm. Leave rem edges unsewn for back V-neck and front edges.•

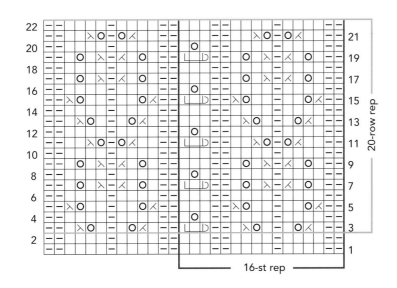

**STITCH KEY**

☐ k on RS, p on WS

⊟ p on RS, k on WS

O yo

⟋ k2tog

⟍ ssk

sl 1, k2, psso

16-st rep

20-row rep

# LACE HOODIE

Multiple patterns of dainty lace make for a delicate zippered hoodie with lightweight warmth. Brooke Nico's design features sleeves knit in the round and finished with embossed ribbing, a hood with a striped lace pattern, and deep slanted pockets.

■■■■▶

### SIZES
Small (Medium, Large). Shown in size Small.

### KNITTED MEASUREMENTS
**Bust** 36 (41, 47)"/91.5 (104, 119.5)cm
**Length** 20 (22, 23)"/51 (56, 58.5)cm
**Upper arm** 12½ (13½, 15)"/31.5 (34.5, 38)cm

### MATERIALS
• 7 (8, 9) .88oz/25g balls (each approx 230yd/210m) of **Valley Yarns** Southampton (kid mohair/silk) in #014 Natural **1**
• One each sizes 1 and 3 (2.25 and 3.25mm) circular needle, each 24"/60cm long, OR SIZE TO OBTAIN GAUGES
• One set (5) each sizes 1 and 3 (2.25 and 3.25mm) double-pointed needles (dpn)
• One size 3 (3.25mm) circular needle, 16"/40cm long
• One size D/3 (3.25mm) crochet hook
• Stitch markers
• Stitch holders
• 20 (22, 23)"/51 (56, 58.5)cm separating zipper
• Sewing needle and matching thread

### GAUGES
• 22 sts and 36 rows to 4"/10cm over charts 3 and 6, after blocking, using larger needles.
• 26 sts and 34 rows/rnds to 4"/10cm over charts 2 and 7, after blocking, using larger needles.
TAKE TIME TO CHECK GAUGES.

### NOTES
**1)** Hoodie is worked from the top down.
**2)** Only RS rows are charted. Purl all WS rows in yoke and body. Knit even rnds in sleeves.
**3)** Bust measurements include front zipper bands measuring approx 1½"/4cm.

### STITCH GLOSSARY
**MC (mock cable)** Pass 3rd st on LH needle over first two sts and off needle, k1, yo, k1.

### BACK
With longer larger needle, cast on 49 (57, 65) sts.
**Set-up row (WS)** P2, pm, p1, pm, p9, pm, p1, pm, p23 (31, 39), pm, p1, pm, p9, pm, p1, pm, p2.

Begin Charts 2 and 3
**Row 1 (RS)** K1, M1, k1, yo, sm, k1, sm, work row 1 of chart 2 to marker, sm, k1, sm, work row 1 of chart 3 to rep line, work 8-st rep 2 (3, 4) times, work to end of chart, sm, k1, sm, work row 1 of chart 2 to marker, sm, k1, sm, yo, k1, M1, k1—59 (67, 75) sts.
**Row 2 and all WS rows (except row 6)** Purl.
**Row 3** K1, M1, k2tog, yo, k1, yo, sm, k1, sm, work chart 2 to marker, sm, k1, sm, work chart 3 to marker, sm, k1, sm, work chart 2 to marker, sm, k1, sm, yo, k1, yo, ssk, M1, k1—69 (77, 85) sts.
**Row 5** K1, M1, k2tog, yo, k3, yo, sm, k1, sm, work chart 2 to marker, sm, k1, sm, work chart 3 to marker, sm, k1, sm, work chart 2 to marker, sm, k1, sm, yo, k3, yo, ssk, M1, k1—79 (87, 95) sts.
**Row 6** P to end, cast on 7 sts—86 (94, 102) sts.
**Row 7** K11, yo, SK2P, yo, k1, yo, sm, k1, sm, work chart 2 to marker, sm, k1, sm, work chart 3 to marker, sm, k1, sm, work chart 2 to marker, sm, k1, sm, yo, k1, yo, SK2P, yo, k4, cast on 7 sts—101 (109, 117) sts.

Begin Charts 1 and 4
**Note** Cont to work charts 2 and 3 as established. Charts 2 and 3 will be on different rows than charts 1 and 4 throughout yoke, keep careful track of rows.
**Row 9** Work row 1 of chart 1, sm, k1, sm, work chart 2 to marker, sm, k1, sm, work chart 3 to marker, sm, k1, sm, work chart 2 to marker, sm, k1, sm, work row 1 of chart 4 to end—109 (117, 125) sts.

row 1 (9, 1) of chart 5 to rep line (end of rep, rep line), work 8-st rep 5 (5, 6) times, work to end of chart.

Cont to work charts as established through row 16 of charts 5 and 6, then work rows 1–16 five times more, and then work rows 0 (1–8, 0) once more—96 chart rows worked.

Change to smaller circular needle.

**Next row (RS)** Knit, dec 2 sts evenly across—193 (217, 241) sts.

**Next row (WS)** P3, *k1, p2; rep from * to last st, p1.

Begin Embossed Rib

**Row 1 (RS)** K3, *yo, k1, yo, k2; rep from * to last st, k1.

**Row 2** P3, *k3tog, p2; rep from * to last st, p1.

Rep rows 1 and 2 for embossed rib 11 times more. Bind off loosely knitwise.

SLEEVES

Place 73 (81, 89) sleeve sts on shorter, larger circular needle. Cast on 4 sts, k across sleeve sts, cast on 4 sts—81 (89, 97) sts. Join and pm for beg of rnd.

Begin Chart 7

**Note** Knit all even rnds. Change to larger dpn when necessary.

**Note** For Medium size only, begin chart 7 with rnd 9.

**Rnd 1** Work to rep line, work 8-st rep 7 (8, 9) times, work to end of chart.

Cont to work chart in this way through rnd 80, then work rnds 1–38 (1–60, 1–62) once more—59 (63, 69) sts.

Change to smaller dpn.

**Next rnd** Knit, dec 2 (3, 3) sts evenly around—57 (60, 66) sts.

Begin Embossed Rib

**Rnd 1** K1, *yo, k1, yo, k2; rep from *, end last rep k1.

**Rnd 2** K1, *p3tog, k2; rep from *, end last rep k1.

Rep rnds 1 and 2 for embossed rib 11 times more. Bind off loosely knitwise.

FRONT ZIPPER BANDS

With RS facing and crochet hook, work 90 (94, 98) single crochet (sc) (see page 165) evenly along right front edge. Work 4 rows more in sc. Fasten off. Rep for left front edge.

Zipper Facing Bands (make 2)

With crochet hook, ch 91 (95, 99) sts. Work 5 rows sc over 90 (94, 98) sts. Fasten off. Set aside.

HOOD

With RS facing and longer larger needle, beg at right front neck edge, pick up and k 50 (54, 58) sts to center back neck, pm, pick up and k 50 (54, 58) sts to left center front neck edge—100 (108, 116) sts.

**Row 11** Work chart 1 to marker, sm, k1, sm, work chart 2 to marker, sm, k1, sm, work chart 3 to marker, sm, k1, sm, work chart 2 to marker, sm, k1, sm, work chart 4 to end—8 sts inc'd. Cont to work charts in this way, working additional 8-st reps each time each chart is worked, until 16 rows of charts 2 and 3 have been worked 3 (4, 4) times, then work rows 1–15 (1–7, 1–15) once more—325 (365, 405) sts.

Divide for sleeves and body

**Next row (WS)** *P to marker, remove marker, p1, remove marker, sl next 73 (81, 89) sts to st holder for sleeve, cast on 4 sts, pm for side seam, cast on 4 sts, rep from * once more, p to end, removing markers—195 (219, 243) sts for body, 97 (113, 129) sts for back, and 49 (53, 57) sts for each front.

Begin Charts 5 and 6

**Note** Be sure to use the correct Chart 6 for your specific size.

**Next row (RS)** Work row 1 (9, 1) of chart 5 to rep line, work 8-st rep 5 (6, 6) times, work last 5 (1, 5) sts of chart, sm, work row 1 (9, 1) of chart 6 to rep line, work 8-st rep 11 (13, 15) times, work to end of chart, sm, beg with st 1 (5, 1), work

## Begin Fagotting

**Rows 1–6** K4, *yo, k2tog, k2; rep from * to end.

**Row 7** K4, *yo, k2tog, k2; rep from * to 2 sts before marker, yo, k2, sm, k2, **yo, k2tog, k2; rep from ** to end—101 (109, 117) sts.

**Row 8** K4, *yo, k2tog, k2; rep from * to 2 sts before marker, yo, k2, sm, k3, **yo, k2tog, k2; rep from ** to end—102 (110, 118) sts.

**Rows 9–14** K4, *yo, k2tog, k2; rep from * to 1 st before marker, k1, sm, k3, **yo, k2tog, k2; rep from ** to end.

**Row 15** K4, *yo, k2tog, k2; rep from * to 3 sts before marker, yo, k3, sm, k3, **yo, k2tog, k2; rep from ** to end—103 (111, 119) sts.

**Row 16** K4, *yo, k2tog, k2; rep from * to 3 sts before marker, yo, k3, sm, **yo, k2tog, k2; rep from ** to end—104 (112, 120) sts.

**Rows 17–22** K4, *yo, k2tog, k2; rep from * to end.

**Row 23** K4, *yo, k2tog, k2; rep from * to marker, sm, k1, yo, k3, **yo, k2tog, k2; rep from ** to end—105 (113, 121) sts.

**Row 24** K4, *yo, k2tog, k2; rep to 1 st before marker, k1, sm, k1, yo, k3, **yo, k2tog, k2; rep from ** to end—106 (114, 122) sts.

**Rows 25–30** K4, *yo, k2tog, k2; rep from * to 1 st before marker, k1, sm, k1, **yo, k2tog, k2; rep from ** to end.

**Row 31** K4, *yo, k2tog, k2; rep from * to 1 st before marker, yo, k1, sm, k1, **yo, k2tog, k2; rep from ** to end—107 (115, 123) sts.

**Row 32** K4, *yo, k2tog, k2; rep from * to 1 st before marker, yo, k1, sm, k2, **yo, k2tog, k2; rep from ** to end—108 (116, 124) sts.

**Rows 33–64** Rep rows 1–32 once more—116 (124, 132) sts.

**Row 65** K4, *yo, k2tog, k2; rep from * to end.

Rep row 65 until hood measures 13"/33cm from beg.

## Top Shaping

**Next row** K4, *yo, k2tog, k2; rep from * to 2 sts before marker, k2tog, sm, k2, **yo, k2tog, k2; rep from ** to end—115 (123, 131) sts.

**Next row** K4, *yo, k2tog, k2; rep from * to 2 sts before marker, k2tog, sm, k1, **yo, k2tog, k2; rep from ** to end—114 (122, 130) sts.

**Next row** K4, *yo, k2tog, k2; rep from * to 5 sts before marker, yo, k2tog, k1, k2tog, sm, k1, **yo, k2tog, k2; rep from ** to end—113 (121, 129) sts.

**Next row** K4, *yo, k2tog, k2; rep from * to 5 sts before marker, yo, k2tog, k1, k2tog, sm, k2tog, k2, **yo, k2tog, k2; rep from ** to end—111 (119, 127) sts.

**Next row** K4, *yo, k2tog, k2; rep from * to 1 st before marker, k1, sm, k2tog, k2, **yo, k2tog, k2; rep from ** to end—110 (118, 126) sts.

**Next row** K4, *yo, k2tog, k2; rep from * to 1 st before marker, k1, sm, k2tog, k1, **yo, k2tog, k2; rep from ** to end—109 (117, 125) sts.

**Next row** K4, *yo, k2tog, k2; rep from * to marker, sm, k2tog, k1, **yo, k2tog, k2; rep from ** to end—108 (116, 124) sts.

Slip 54 (58, 62) sts to spare needle and loosely work 3-needle bind-off (see page 164) to join top of hood.

## RIGHT POCKET

With larger needle, cast on 59 (67, 79) sts. Purl 1 row.

## Begin Smocked Lace Stitch

**Row 1 (RS)** K2, *MC, k1; rep from * to last st, k1.

**Row 2** Purl.

**Row 3** K4, *MC, k1; rep from * to last 3 sts, k3.

**Row 4** Purl.

Rep rows 1–4 four times more, then rep rows 1 and 2 once more.

**Row 23** K4, *MC, k1; rep from * to last 3 sts, k2tog, k1—1 st dec'd.

**Row 24 and all WS rows** Purl.

**Row 25** K2, *MC, k1; rep from * to last 4 sts, k1, k2tog, k1—1 st dec'd.

**Row 27** K4, *MC, k1; rep from * to last 5 sts, k2, k2tog, k1—1 st dec'd.

**Row 29** K2, *MC, k1; rep from * to last 6 sts, MC, k2tog, k1—1 st dec'd.

**Row 30** Purl.

Rep rows 23–30 for 5 (5, 6) times more—35 (43, 51) sts.
Bind off loosely knitwise.

## LEFT POCKET

With larger needle, cast on 59 (67, 79) sts. Purl 1 row.
Work rows 1–22 as for right pocket.

**Row 23** K1, ssk, k1, *MC, k1; rep from * to last 3 sts, k3—1 st dec'd.

**Row 24 and all WS rows** Purl.

**Row 25** K1, ssk, k2, *MC, k1; rep from * to last st, k1—1 st dec'd.

**Row 27** K1, ssk, k3, *MC, k1; rep from * to last 3 sts, k3—1 st dec'd.

**Row 29** K1, ssk, *MC, k1; rep from * to last st, k1—1 st dec'd.

**Row 30** Purl.

Rep rows 23–30 for 5 (5, 6) times more—35 (43, 51) sts.
Bind off loosely knitwise.

## FINISHING

Sew underarm seams. Weave in ends. Block to measurements. Block pockets and zipper facing bands. Sew pockets to fronts, placing cast-on edge at the upper edge of ribbing and long side seam along front zipper band seam.

Pin zipper in place along center fronts, making sure that front lays flat. Sew zipper in place. Pin zipper facing bands to wrong side of fronts, covering zipper tape. Sew facing bands in place, ensuring that fronts remain flat.•

## CHART 6 (SMALL AND LARGE SIZES ONLY)

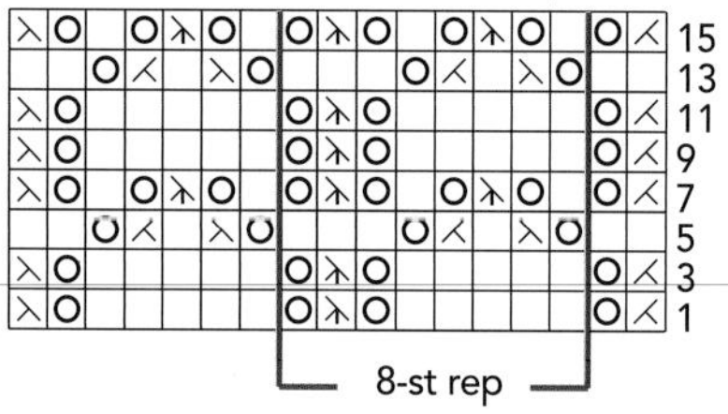

8-st rep

## STITCH KEY

| | k on RS, p on WS |
|---|---|
| ⟋ | k2tog |
| ⟍ | ssk |
| O | yo |
| ⋏ | SK2P |

**Note** Only the RS is charted.
Purl even rows. Knit even rnds.

## CHART 6 (MEDIUM SIZE ONLY)

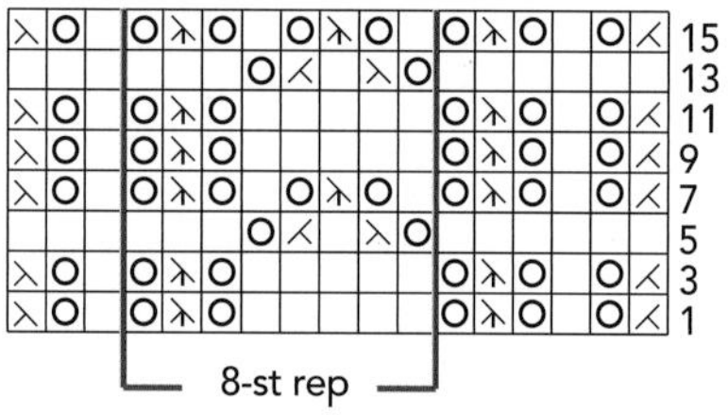

8-st rep

## CHART 5

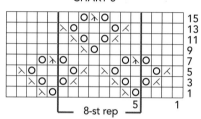

8-st rep

## CHART 4

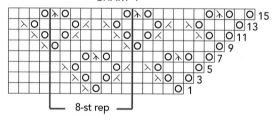

8-st rep

## CHART 1

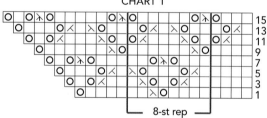

8-st rep

## CHART 3

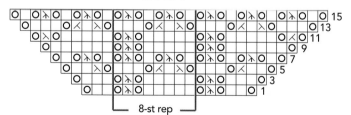

8-st rep

## CHART 2

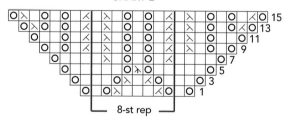

8-st rep

## CHART 7

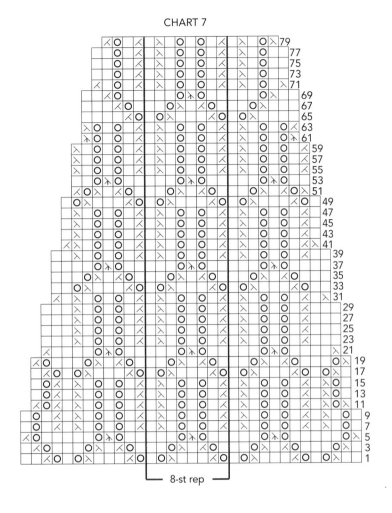

8-st rep

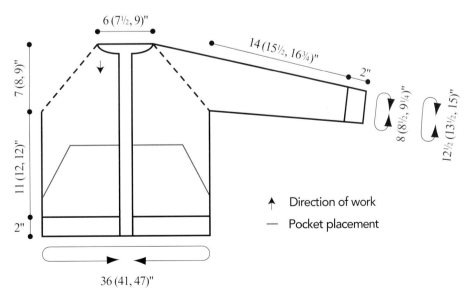

6 (7½, 9)"

14 (15½, 16¾)"

2"

7 (8, 9)"

8 (8½, 9¼)"

12½ (13½, 15)"

11 (12, 12)"

2"

↑  Direction of work

—  Pocket placement

36 (41, 47)"

# COUNTERPANE-INSPIRED SHAWL

If ever there were a statement shawl, Jacqueline van Dillen's lavishly sized wrap, with elegance that belies its simplicity, is it. Six squares (knit in the round) and four triangles (knit back and forth in rows) are joined with a three-needle bind-off along adjacent sides before long, breezy fringe is attached during finishing.

◼◼◼▬

## KNITTED MEASUREMENTS
**Width (at widest point)** 74"/188cm
**Length (center back to point)** 46.5"/118cm

## MATERIALS
• Original Yarn
8  3½oz/100g skeins (each approx 170yd/155m) of **Fibra Natura/Universal Yarn** Good Earth Solids (cotton/linen) in #105 Petal (4)
• Substitute Yarn
15  1¾oz/50g balls, (each approx 92yd/83m) of **Valley Yarns** Goshen (Peruvian cotton/modal/silk) in #30 Light Pink (4)
• One set (5) size 7 (4.5mm) double-pointed needles (dpn), OR SIZE TO OBTAIN GAUGES
• One size 7 (4.5mm) circular needle, 40"/100cm long
• One size 7 (4.5mm) crochet hook
• Stitch markers
• Stitch holders

## GAUGES
• 16 sts and 20 rows to 4"/10cm over St st using size 7 (4.5mm) needles.
• One square is approx 15"/38cm square using size 7 (4.5mm) needles.
TAKE TIME TO CHECK GAUGES.

## CIRCULAR CAST-ON
**1)** Wrap the yarn loosely around 2 fingers, the loose tail near your fingertips and the working yarn to the inside.
**2)** With a crochet hook, bring the working strand under the inside strand, then draw the loop through.
**3)** Draw through another loop to complete the stitch. Repeat steps 2 and 3 until desired number of sts have been cast on. Place sts on straight needle or distribute them over dpn. Close ring by pulling the loose tail.

## STITCH GLOSSARY
**M3** With needle tip, lift strand between last st knit and next st on LH needle, (k1, p1, k1) into this strand—3 sts inc'd.
**M4** With needle tip, lift strand between last st knit and next st on LH needle, (k1, p1, k1, p1) into this strand—4 sts inc'd.
**M6** With needle tip, lift strand between last st knit and next st on LH needle, (k1, p1, k1, p1, k1, p1) into this strand—6 sts inc'd.

## NOTES
**1)** The shawl is made of 6 squares (knit from center out in the round) and 4 triangles (worked back and forth in rows).
**2)** Begin with one triangle with subsequent squares and triangles joined using a 3-needle bind-off (see diagram).

## SHAWL
Triangle 1
Cast on 10 sts using circular cast-on. Place sts on circular needle. Work back and forth in rows as foll:

Begin chart 1
**Note** Chart 1 is split in half. Work both halves each row.
Begin with row 1 on WS, work rows 1–38 of chart—98 sts.
Place markers on each side of 2 center k sts.
**Next row (WS)** Purl.
**Next row (RS)** K2, yo, k to marker, yo, sm, k2, sm, yo, k to last 2 sts, yo, k2.
Rep last 2 rows 5 times more—122 sts.
Purl 1 row.
Bind off 61 sts, place rem 61 sts on holder.

ROSE CALLAHAN

## CHART 1 - LEFT HALF

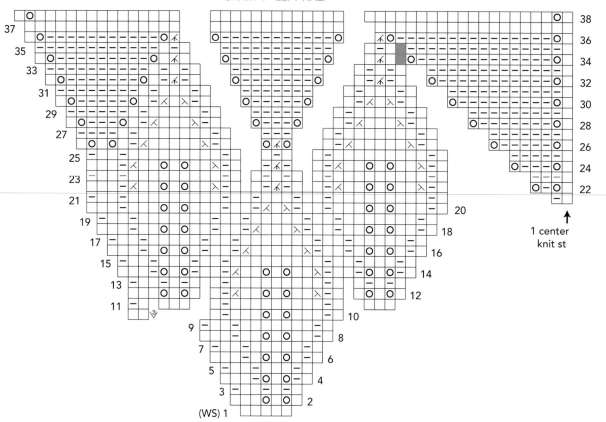

1 center
knit st

50

CHART 1 - RIGHT HALF

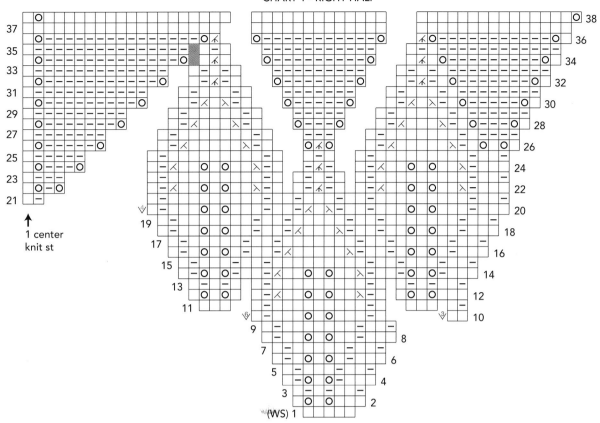

**STITCH KEY**

| □ | k on RS, p on WS | ▨ | no stitch |
|---|---|---|---|
| ─ | p on RS, k on WS | ⋏ | k3tog on RS |
| ○ | yo | ⩔ | M3 |
| ⋏ | k2tog on RS | ⩔ | M4 |
| ⋋ | ssk on RS | ⩔ | M6 |

Square 2
Cast on 12 sts using circular cast-on. Divide sts evenly over 4 dpn. Join, taking care not to twist sts, and cont in the rnd as foll:

Begin chart 2
**Rnd 1** Knit.
**Rnd 2** [K1, yo, k1, yo, k1] 4 times.
Cont in chart as established through row 38, changing to circular needle and placing a marker between sts from each dpn when sts no longer fit comfortably on dpn—212 sts. Mark the 2 center k sts in each rep.
**Next rnd** Knit.
**Inc rnd** [K to 2 corner sts, yo, k2, yo] 4 times, k to end—8 sts inc'd.
Rep last 2 rnds 3 times more—244 sts.

Joining
Bind off 61 sts, work 3-needle bind-off (see page 164) with the next 61 sts and the 61 sts from previous triangle, place rem 122 sts on a holder.

Cont to make squares and triangles as established, joining as you go foll diagram.

FINISHING
Weave in ends. Block to measurements.

Border
Cast on 13 sts.
**Row 1 (RS)** K13.
**Row 2 (WS)** Pick up a st along upper edge of shawl (see diagram), p2tog (picked-up st and first st of border), p9, k3. Turn work.
**Row 3 (RS)** K13.
Rep last 2 rows evenly along edge, end with a knit row.
Bind off.

Fringe (make 65)
Cut strands of yarn each approx 16"/40cm long. With 2 strands held tog for each fringe, use crochet hook to attach evenly along other two sides.•

# CHART 2

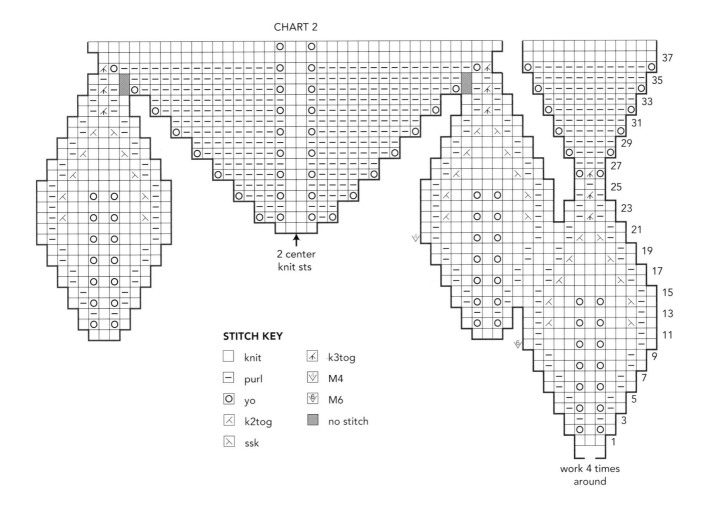

2 center
knit sts

**STITCH KEY**

| | | | |
|---|---|---|---|
| ☐ | knit | ⟁ | k3tog |
| ⊟ | purl | ⱱ | M4 |
| ⊙ | yo | ⑥ | M6 |
| ⟋ | k2tog | ▨ | no stitch |
| ⟍ | ssk | | |

work 4 times
around

37
35
33
31
29
27
25
23
21
19
17
15
13
11
9
7
5
3
1

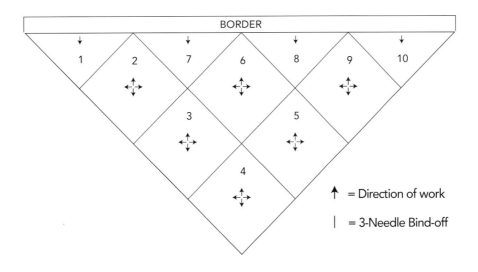

BORDER

↑ = Direction of work

| = 3-Needle Bind-off

# DIAMOND BANDS WRAP

Mesh columns and diamonds work their way across Kirsten Kapur's dramatic lace wrap. Knit in two pieces that are joined at the center with Kitchener stitch, this shawl features garter-stitch trim to ensure that the draping falls just so.

### KNITTED MEASUREMENTS
Approx 24 x 80"/61 x 203cm

### MATERIALS
• Original Yarn
6 3½oz/100g hanks (each approx 150yd/137m) of **Malabrigo Yarn** Twist (wool) in #416 Indiecita (4)
• Substitute Yarn
5 3½oz/100g hanks (each approx 210yd/192m) of **Malabrigo Yarn** Rios (wool) in #416 Indiecita (4)
• Two size 10½ (6.5mm) circular needles, each 32"/80cm long, OR SIZE TO OBTAIN GAUGE
• Stitch markers
• Tapestry needle

### GAUGE
12 sts and 19 rows to 4"/10cm over St st using size 10½ (6.5mm) needles.
TAKE TIME TO CHECK GAUGE.

### NOTES
**1)** Wrap is worked in two halves and joined at center back.
**2)** Alternate skeins every 2 rows to avoid pooling.
**3)** Circular needle is used to accommodate the large number of sts. Do not join.

### WRAP
**First Half**
Cast on 75 sts.
**Row 1 (RS)** Sl 1 wyif, k to end.
Rep row 1 for 15 rows more.

**Begin chart 1**
**Row 1 (RS)** Work to rep line, work 22-st rep twice, work sts after rep to end of chart.
Cont to work chart 1 in this way until rows 1–24 have been worked twice.

**Begin chart 2**
**Row 1 (RS)** Work to rep line, work 22-st rep twice, work sts after rep to end of chart.
Cont to work chart 2 in this way through row 14, then rep rows 13 and 14 only 41 times more.

**Begin chart 3**
**Row 1 (RS)** Work to rep line, work 22-st rep twice, work sts after rep to end of chart.
Cont to work chart 3 in this way through row 9.
Cut yarn leaving long tail for grafting. Set aside first half.

**Second Half**
Work as for first half.

### FINISHING
Using long tail and with RS facing, graft tog halves using Kitchener stitch (see page 164).
Weave in ends. Block lightly to measurements.•

## CHART 1

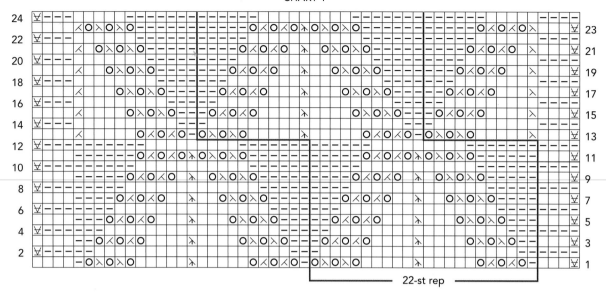

22-st rep

## CHART 2

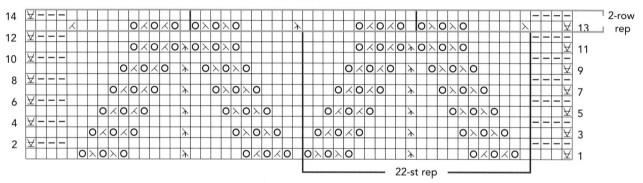

2-row rep

22-st rep

## CHART 3

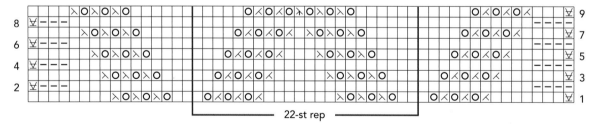

22-st rep

**STITCH KEY**

☐ k on RS, p on WS    ⩔ slip 1 wyif    ⋏ SK2P    ⟍ ssk

⊟ p on RS, k on WS    ⊙ yo    ⟋ k2tog

# GREYSTONE HARBOR SHAWL

Rosemary (Romi) Hill's oversized wrap is just the thing when the evening calls for drama. Garland-like columns are interspersed with double lines across the asymmetrical triangle, which increases from one point, making the size easy to alter. Gentle scallops form organically along the self-finished edges.

### KNITTED MEASUREMENTS
**Width (upper edge)** Approx 68"/172.5cm
**Length (at center)** Approx 34"/86.5cm

### MATERIALS
• Original Yarn
7  1¾oz/50g hanks (each approx
150yd/137m) of **Classic Elite Yarns** Canyon
(cotton/alpaca) in #3703 Mesquite (2)
• Substitute Yarn
7  1¾oz/50g hanks (each approx
167yd150m) of **Valley Yarns** Granville
(pima cotton/merino wool) in
#04 Silver (2)
• One size 6 (4mm) circular needle
32"/80cm long, OR SIZE TO OBTAIN GAUGE

### GAUGE
17 sts and 23 rows to 4"/10cm over chart
pats using size 6 (4mm) needles.
TAKE TIME TO CHECK GAUGE.

### STRETCHY BIND-OFF
K2, *sl 2 sts back to LH needle, k2tog tbl, k1; rep from * to end, sl 2 sts back to LH needle, k2tog tbl, fasten off last st.

### SHAWL
Cast on 3 sts.
**Row 1** Kfb, k1, kfb—5 sts.
**Row 2** *K1 tbl; rep from * to end.

Begin Chart 1
Work chart 1 through row 38—35 sts.

Begin Chart 2
**Row 1 (RS)** Work to rep line, skip 17-st rep, work sts after rep to end of row.
Cont to work chart 2 in this way through row 24—52 sts.
**Row 1 (RS)** Work to rep line, work 17-st rep once, work sts after rep to end of row.

Cont to work chart 2 in this way until 24 rows of chart have been worked, then work chart 9 times more (11 times total), working 1 more 17-st rep each time—222 sts.

Begin Chart 3
**Row 1 (RS)** Work to rep line, work 17-st rep 11 times, work sts after rep to end of row.
Work chart 3 in this way through row 12—258 sts.
Bind off using stretchy bind-off.

FINISHING
Weave in ends. Block to measurements, pinning out points.•

## STITCH KEY

| | | | |
|---|---|---|---|
| □ | k on RS, p on WS | ℚ | k1 tbl on WS |
| − | p on RS, k on WS | ⧄ | k2tog |
| ▨ | no stitch | ⧅ | ssk |
| ○ | yo | ⧄ | k2tog tbl |
| ℚ | k1 tbl on RS | ⅗ | (k1, yo, k1) in same st |

CHART 1

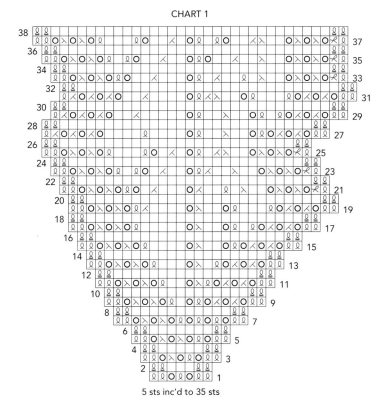

5 sts inc'd to 35 sts

CHART 2

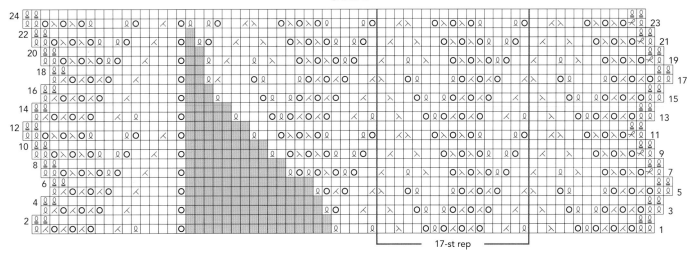

17-st rep

CHART 3

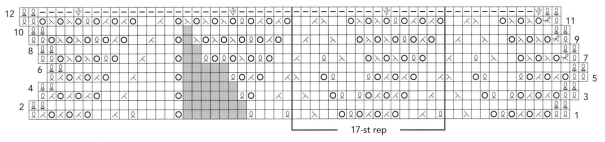

17-st rep

# DEEP V-NECK DUSTER

Diamond lace patterns in a trio of sizes and divided by garter bands adorn Deborah Newton's longline closure-free cardigan, with the loose fit and open front contributing to the elevated loungewear look. Wide eyelet-garter borders around the edges are in keeping with an overall airiness.

■■■□

## SIZES
Small (Medium, Large, X-Large, XX-Large).
Shown in size Small.

## KNITTED MEASUREMENTS
**Bust (closed)** 38½ (41½, 44, 47, 50)"/98 (105.5, 111.5, 119, 127)cm
**Length** 28¾ (29¼, 29¾, 30¾, 31¼)"/73 (74, 75.5, 78, 79.5)cm
**Upper arm** 14 (15, 16, 17½, 18½)"/35.5 (38, 40.5, 44.5, 47)cm

## MATERIALS
• Original Yarn
9 (10, 11, 12, 13) 1¾oz/50g balls (each approx 137yd/125m) of **Classic Elite Yarns** Soft Linen (wool/linen/alpaca) in #2249 Tropical Sea (2)
• Substitute Yarn
9 (10, 11, 12, 13) 1¾oz/50g balls (each approx 137yd/125m) of **Rowan** Alpaca Soft DK (wool/alpaca) in #217 Naples Blue (2)
• One pair size 6 (4mm) needles, OR SIZE TO OBTAIN GAUGES
• One size 6 (4mm) circular needle, 32"/90cm long
• Stitch markers

## GAUGES
• 18 sts and 32 rows to 4"/10cm over chart 1 using size 6 (4mm) needles.
• 17 sts and 28 rows to 4"/10cm over chart 3 using size 6 (4mm) needles.
TAKE TIME TO CHECK GAUGES.

## NOTE
The lower edge lace trim is picked up and knit down from the finished back and front pieces and finished sleeves. This edge is not included on the schematics.

## BACK
Cast on 83 (89, 95, 101, 107) sts.

### Begin Chart 1
**Row 1 (WS)** P2 (selvage sts), pm, p to last 2 sts, pm, p2 (selvage sts).
**Row 2 (RS)** K2 (selvage sts), sm, work first st of row 2 of chart 1, work 6-st rep 12 (13, 14, 15, 16) times, work last 6 sts of chart 1, sm, k2 (selvage sts).
Cont to foll chart 1 in this way until 48 rows (or 6 reps of 8-row pat rep) are worked.
Knit 7 rows.

### Begin Chart 2
Beg with row 2 of chart 2 as foll:
**Chart row 2 (RS)** K2, sm, work first 3 sts of row 2 of chart 2, work 6-st rep 12 (13, 14, 15, 16) times, work the last 4 sts of chart 2, sm, k2.
Cont to foll chart 2 in this way until 50 rows (or 5 reps of 10-row pat rep) are worked.
Knit 7 rows, inc 1 st at center of last WS row—84 (90, 96, 102, 108) sts.

### Begin Chart 3
Beg with row 2 of chart 3 as foll:
**Chart row 2 (RS)** K2, sm, work first st of row 2 of chart 3, work the 6-st rep 13 (14, 15, 16, 17) times, work the last st of the chart, sm, k2.
Work even in pat until 18 rows of chart 3 are worked.
Piece measures approx 17"/43cm from beg.

### Armhole Shaping
**Note** When working armhole shaping in chart 3 pat, discontinue k2 selvage sts and work sts in plain St st (k on RS, p on WS) when there are not enough sts to work eyelet lace pat.
Bind off 5 sts at beg of next 2 rows.
**Dec row (RS)** Ssk, work pat to last 2 sts, k2tog.
Rep dec row ever other row 5 (7, 9, 11, 13) times more—62 (64, 66, 68, 70) sts.

Work even until armhole measures 7½ (8, 8½, 9½, 10)"/19 (20.5, 21.5, 24, 25.5)cm.
On the last WS row, pm to mark center 12 (12, 12, 14, 14) sts.

## Neck and Shoulder Shaping

**Next row (RS)** Bind off 5 (6, 5, 5, 6) sts, work to center marked sts, join a 2nd ball of yarn and bind off center 12 (12, 12, 14, 14) sts, work to end.
Cont to shape shoulder, binding off 5 (6, 5, 5, 6) sts from beg of next WS row then bind off 5 (5, 6, 6, 6) sts from each shoulder edge twice more, AT THE SAME TIME, bind off 5 sts from each neck edge twice.

## LEFT FRONT

Cast on 41 (47, 47, 53, 53) sts.

### Begin Chart 1

**Row 1 (WS)** P2 (selvage sts), pm, p to last 2 sts, pm, p2 (selvage sts).
**Row 2 (RS)** K2 (selvage sts), sm, work first st of row 2 of chart, work 6-st rep 5 (6, 6, 7, 7) times, work the last 6 sts of chart, sm, k2 (selvage sts).
Cont to foll chart 1 in this way until 48 rows (or 6 reps of 8-row pat rep) are worked.
Knit 7 rows.

### Begin Chart 2

Beg with row 2 of chart 2 as foll:
**Chart row 2 (RS)** K2, sm, work first 3 sts of row 2 of chart, work the 6-st rep 5 (6, 6, 7, 7) times, work last 4 sts of chart, sm, k2.
Cont to foll chart 2 in this way until 50 rows of 10-row pat rep are worked.
Knit 7 rows, inc 1 st at center on last WS row—42 (48, 48, 54, 54) sts.

### Begin Chart 3

Beg with row 2 of chart 3 as foll:
**Chart row 2 (RS)** K2, sm, work first st of row 2 of chart 3, work the 6-st rep 6 (7, 7, 8, 8) times, work the last st of chart, sm, k2.
Work even foll chart 3 until piece measures 15"/38cm from beg.

### Neck Shaping

**Dec row (RS)** Work pat to last 2 sts, k2tog.
Place marker to mark beg of neck shaping on this row.
Rep dec row every 4th row 15 (16, 15, 14, 14) times more then every 2nd row 0 (2, 0, 5, 2) times, AT THE SAME TIME, when piece measures same length as back to armhole, work as foll:

### Armhole Shaping

**Next row (RS)** Bind off 5 sts, work to end.

Cont with the neck shaping, dec 1 st at armhole edge by working ssk at beg of every RS row 6 (8, 10, 12, 14) times. After all shaping, work even on rem 15 (16, 17, 17, 18) sts until armhole measures 7½ (8, 8½, 9½, 10)"/19 (20.5, 21.5, 24, 25.5)cm.

### Shoulder shaping

Bind off 5 (6, 5, 5, 6) sts from armhole edge once, then 5 (5, 6, 6, 6) sts twice.

## RIGHT FRONT

Work as for left front, reversing all shaping.

## SLEEVES

Cast on 35 (41, 41, 47, 47) sts.

### Begin Chart 2

**Row 1 (WS)** P2 (selvage sts), pm, p to last 2 sts, pm, p2 (selvage sts).
**Row 2 (RS)** K2, sm, work first 3 sts of row 2 of chart 2, work 6-st rep 4 (5, 5, 6, 6) times, work last 4 sts of chart 2, sm, k2. Cont to work in this way until 40 rows (or 4 reps of 10-row pat) are completed.
Knit 7 rows.
**Next row (RS)** Knit, inc 7 sts evenly spaced across row—42 (48, 48, 54, 54) sts.

### Begin Chart 3

**Chart row 1 (WS)** P2, sm, p to last 2 sts, sm, p2.
**Chart row 2 (RS)** K2, sm, work first st of row 2 of chart 3, work 6-st rep 6 (7, 7, 8, 8) times, work last st of chart 3, sm, k2.
Work even foll chart for 3 rows more.
**Inc row (RS)** K2, sm, M1, work to next marker, M1, sm, k2.
Rep inc row every 8th row 6 (6, 0, 0, 0) times more, every 6th row 3 (2, 10, 10, 12) times—62 (66, 70, 76, 80) sts.
Work even until piece measures approx 16½ (16½, 16½, 16¾, 16¾)"/42 (42, 42, 42.5, 42.5)cm from beg.

### Cap Shaping

**Note** When working cap shaping in chart 3 pat, discontinue k2 selvage sts and work sts in plain St st when there are not sufficient sts to work eyelet lace pat.
Bind off 5 sts at beg of next 2 rows.
**Dec row (RS)** Ssk, work pat to last 2 sts, k2tog.
Rep dec row every other row 15 (17, 19, 22, 24) times more—20 sts. Bind off.

### Sleeve Cuff Trim

With RS facing, pick up and k 35 (41, 41, 47, 47) sts along cast-on edge of sleeve. Knit 3 rows.
**Eyelet row (RS)** K1, *yo, k2tog, k1; rep from * to last st, k1.
Purl 1 row. Knit 4 rows. Bind off.

## FINISHING

Block pieces lightly on WS to measurements.
Sew shoulder seams. Set in sleeves, easing to fit if necessary.
Sew sleeve seams. Sew side seams.

### Lower Edge Trim

With circular needle and RS facing, pick up and k 158 (176, 182, 200, 206) sts evenly along lower edge of left front, back and right front (approx 1 st for every st along cast-on edge).
**Rows 1–3** Knit.
**Eyelet row 4 (RS)** K1, *yo, k2tog, k1; rep from * to last st, k1.
**Row 5** Purl.
**Rows 6–9** Knit.
**Rows 10 and 11** Rep rows 4 and 5.
Knit 8 rows. [Rep rows 4 and 5. Knit 4 rows] twice.
Bind off firmly.

### Front Edge Trim

With circular needle and RS facing, pick up and k 95 sts to neck marker, pm, pick up and k 50 (52, 55, 59, 62) sts to shoulder, 42 (41, 41, 45, 45) sts across back neck, 50 (52, 55, 59, 62) sts to neck marker, pm, 95 sts to end—332 (335, 341, 353, 359) sts. Work same as for lower edge, only on all RS garter st rows (excluding eyelet rows), work M1 after first neck marker and M1 st before 2nd neck marker and work inc sts into eyelet pat. Bind off firmly.

Weave in ends.•

CHART 3

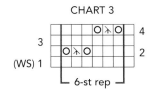

CHART 2

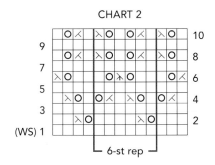

CHART 1

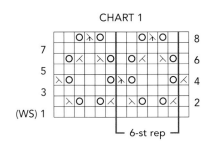

**STITCH KEY**

☐ k on RS, p on WS        ⊙ yo

⟋ k2tog        ⼊ SK2P

⟍ ssk

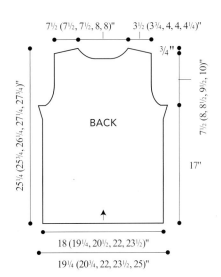

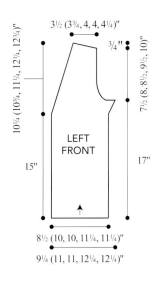

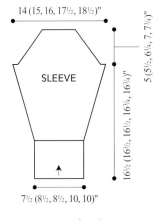

↑ = Direction of work

# DIAMOND-TRIMMED CARDI

For the subtle embellishment of this classic cardigan, beads are pre-strung onto the strand and knit in using slipped stitches, punctuating each diamond lace motif across the waistband, sleeve cuffs, and deep-V neckband. Sarah Hatton's stylish design is worked in pieces and sewn in finishing.

## SIZES
Small (Medium, Large, X-Large, XX-Large).
Shown in size Small.

## KNITTED MEASUREMENTS
**Bust** 32¾ (36¾, 40¾, 44½, 48½)"/83 (93.5, 103.5, 113, 123)cm
**Length** 21½ (22, 22½, 23, 23½)"/54.5 (56, 57, 58.5, 59.5)cm
**Upper arm** 13½ (14¼, 15, 15¾, 16½)"/34.5 (36, 38, 40, 42)cm

## MATERIALS
• Original Yarn
5 (6, 7, 8, 8) 1¾oz/50g skeins (each approx 142yd/130m) of **Rowan** Pure Linen (linen) in #399 Patagonian (3)
• Substitute Yarn
5 (6, 7, 7, 8) 1¾oz/50g balls (each approx 164yd/150m) of **Katia** Lino (linen) in #19 Light Jeans (3)
• One pair each sizes 3 and 5 (3.25 and 3.75mm) needles, OR SIZE TO OBTAIN GAUGE
• One size 3 (3.25mm) circular needle, 40"/100cm long
• Five 1"/25mm buttons
• Approx 102 (113, 123, 134, 144) Rowan/Swarovski Classic Crystal 6mm in Aquamarine #9825101-0008
• Stitch markers

## GAUGE
21 sts and 28 rows to 4"/10cm over St st using larger needles.
TAKE TIME TO CHECK GAUGE.

## NOTE
Do not place beads on final repeat of row 15 on back and each front.

## STITCH GLOSSARY
**place bead** Bring yarn forward, slide bead up to st just worked on RH needle, sl next st, bring yarn to back, ready to work next st.

## BEADS
Pre-string beads onto yarn before working each piece as foll:
**Back** 37 (42, 47, 52, 57) beads
**Left Front/Right Front** 17 (20, 22, 25, 27) beads
**Sleeve** 1 bead
**Neckband** 29 (29, 30, 30, 31) beads

## BACK
With smaller needles, cast on 83 (93, 103, 113, 123) sts.
**Row 1 (RS)** K1, *p1, k1; rep from * to end.
**Row 2** P1, *k1, p1; rep from * to end.
Rep last 2 rows for k1, p1 rib for 4 times more.
Change to larger needles.

### Begin Chart 1
**Row 1 (RS)** Work to rep line, work 10-st rep 7 (8, 9, 10, 11) times, work to end of chart.
Cont to work chart in this way through row 16, then work rows 5–16 twice more.
Beg with a knit row, work in St st (k on RS, p on WS) until piece measures 14"/35.5cm from beg, end with a WS row.

### Armhole Shaping
Bind off 5 (5, 6, 7, 8) sts at beg of next 2 rows.
**Dec row (RS)** K2, SKP, k to last 4 sts, k2tog, k2—2 sts dec'd.
Rep dec row every other row 3 (5, 7, 8, 9) times more—65 (71, 75, 81, 87) sts.
Cont in St st until armhole measures 7 (7½, 8, 8½, 9)"/18 (19, 20.5, 21.5, 23)cm, end with a WS row.
Mark center 27 (29, 31, 33, 35) sts.

## Neck and Shoulder Shaping
**Row 1 (RS)** Bind off 7 (8, 9, 10, 11) sts, work to center marked sts, join 2nd ball of yarn and bind off center 27 (29, 31, 33, 35) sts, work to end.
**Row 2 (WS)** Bind off 7 (8, 9, 10, 11) sts, work to end of first side; bind off 4 sts at neck edge of 2nd side, work to end.
**Row 3** Bind off 8 (9, 9, 10, 11) sts; bind off 4 sts at neck edge of 2nd side, work to end.
**Row 4** Bind off 8 (9, 9, 10, 11) sts.

## LEFT FRONT
With smaller needles, cast on 42 (48, 52, 58, 62) sts.
**Row 1 (RS)** *K1, p1; rep from * to end.
Cont in k1, p1 rib as established for 9 rows more, inc 1 (0, 1, 0, 1) st on last row—43 (48, 53, 58, 63) sts.
Change to larger needles.

### Begin Chart 1
**For sizes Small, Large, and XX-Large only**
**Row 1 (RS)** Work chart to rep line, work 10-st rep 3 (4, 5) times, work to end.

**For sizes Medium and X-Large only**
**Note** In row 9, work first st of first repeat as a k2tog instead of SK2P.
**Row 1 (RS)** K1 (St st edge st), beg at rep line, work 10-st rep 4 (5) times, work to end of chart.

**For all sizes**
Cont to work chart in this way through row 16, then work rows 5–16 twice more.
Beg with a knit row, work in St st until piece measures 12 (12½, 13, 13½, 13½)"/30.5 (31.5, 33, 34.5, 34.5)cm from beg, end with a WS row.

### Neck and Armhole Shaping
**Note** Armhole and neck shaping happen simultaneously, read before cont to knit.
**Neck dec row (RS)** K to last 4 sts, k2tog, k2—1 st dec'd.
Rep neck dec row every other row 10 (11, 12, 13, 14) times, then every 4th row 8 times, AT THE SAME TIME, when piece measures 14"/35.5cm from beg, end with a WS row and shape armhole at side edge as foll:
Bind off 5 (5, 6, 7, 8) sts at beg of next row. Work 1 WS row.
**Dec row (RS)** K2, SKP, k to end—1 st dec'd.
Rep dec at armhole edge every other row 3 (5, 7, 8, 9) times more—15 (17, 18, 20, 22) sts when all shaping is complete.
Cont in St st until armhole measures 7 (7½, 8, 8½, 9)"/18 (19, 20.5, 21.5, 23)cm, end with a WS row. Bind off 7 (8, 9, 10, 11) sts at armhole edge once, 8 (9, 9, 10, 11) sts once.

## RIGHT FRONT
With smaller needles, cast on 42 (48, 52, 58, 62) sts.
**Row 1 (RS)** *P1, k1; rep from * to end.
Cont in k1, p1 rib as established for 9 rows more, inc 1 (0, 1, 0, 1) st on last row—43 (48, 53, 58, 63) sts.
Change to larger needles.

### Begin Chart 1
**For sizes Small, Large, and XX-Large only**
**Row 1 (RS)** Work chart to rep line, work 10-st rep 3 (4, 5) times, work to end.

**For sizes Medium and X-Large only**
**Note** In row 9, work last dec foll last rep as an ssk instead of SK2P.
**Row 1 (RS)** Work chart to rep line, work 10-st rep 4 (5) times, k2 (St st edge sts).

**For all sizes**
Cont to work chart in this way through row 16, then work rows 5–16 twice more.
Beg with a knit row, work in St st until piece measures 12 (12½, 13, 13½, 13½)"/30.5 (31.5, 33, 34.5, 34.5)cm from beg, end with a WS row.

### Neck and Armhole Shaping
**Note** Armhole and neck shaping happen simultaneously, read before cont to knit.
**Neck dec row (RS)** K2, SKP, k to end—1 st dec'd.
Rep neck dec row every other row 10 (11, 12, 13, 14) times, then every 4th row 8 times, AT THE SAME TIME, when piece measures 14"/35.5cm from beg, end with a RS row and shape armhole at side edge as foll:
Bind off 5 (5, 6, 7, 8) sts at beg of next row.
**Dec row (RS)** K to last 4 sts, k2tog, k2—1 st dec'd.
Rep dec at armhole edge every other row 3 (5,7, 8, 9) times more—15 (17, 18, 20, 22) sts when all shaping is complete.
Cont in St st until armhole measures 7 (7½, 8, 8½, 9)"/18 (19, 20.5, 21.5, 23)cm, end with a RS row. Bind off 7 (8, 9, 10, 11) sts at armhole edge once, 8 (9, 9, 10, 11) sts once.

## SLEEVES
With smaller needles, cast on 47 (47, 51, 51, 53) sts. Work 6 rows in k1, p1 rib as for back.
Change to larger needles.
Beg with a knit row, work 2 rows in St st.

### Begin Chart 2
**Row 1 (RS)** K18 (18, 20, 20, 21), pm, work 11 sts of chart 2, pm, k to end.
Cont to work chart 2 in this way through row 16, then cont in St st, AT THE SAME TIME, inc 1 st each side on next RS row,

then every 6th (6th, 6th, 4th, 4th) row 8 (13, 13, 5, 8) times,
then every 8th (0, 0, 6th, 6th) row 3 (0, 0, 10, 8) times—71 (75, 79, 83, 87) sts.
Work even in St st until piece measures 13 (13½, 13½, 14, 14)"/33 (34.5, 34.5, 35.5, 5.5)cm from beg, end with a WS row.

Cap Shaping
Bind off 5 (5, 6, 7, 8) sts at beg of next 2 rows.
**Dec row (RS)** K2, SKP, k to last 4 sts, k2tog, k2—2 sts dec'd.
Rep dec row every other row 3 (5, 7, 8, 9) times more.
Work 1 WS row.
Bind off 7 sts at beg of next 6 rows.
Bind off rem 11 (11, 9, 9, 9) sts.

FINISHING
Weave in ends. Block pieces to measurements. Sew shoulder seams. Set in sleeves. Sew side and sleeve seams.

Neckband
With circular needle and RS facing, pick up and k 75 (77, 81, 85, 85) sts along right front edge to beg of neck shaping, pm, 55 (55, 55, 55, 57) sts along right front neck edge, 35 (37, 39, 41, 43) sts along back neck edge, 55 (55, 55, 55, 57) sts along left front neck edge, pm, 75 (77, 81, 85, 85) sts along left front edge to lower edge—295 (301, 311, 321, 327) sts.
**Row 1 (WS)** P1, *k1, p1; rep from * to end.
**Row 2 (RS)** Work in rib to first marker, sm, work 2 (3, 2, 3, 3) in rib, [place bead, rib 4] 28 (28, 29, 29, 30) times, place bead, rib to end.
Work 1 WS row in rib.
**Buttonhole row (RS)** Rib 3 (5, 3, 5, 5), [k2tog, yo, rib 14 (14, 16, 16, 16)] 4 times, k2tog, yo, rib to end.
Work 3 rows more in rib. Bind off in rib.
Sew buttons to left front band opposite buttonholes.•

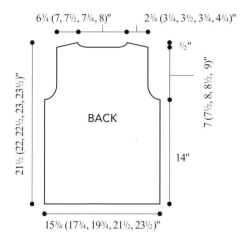

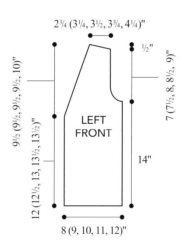

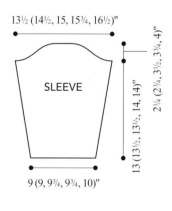

CHART 1

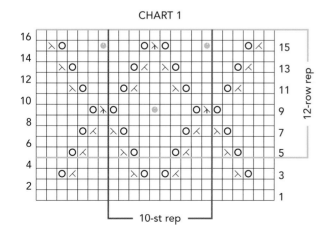

CHART 2

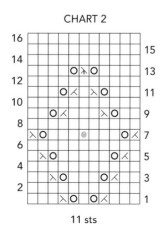

**STITCH KEY**

☐ k on RS, p on WS

⧄ k2tog

⧅ ssk

☐ yo

⋏ SK2P

⬤ place bead

# BEADED CRESCENT SHAWL

Anniken Allis embellishes three cascading lace patterns with beads for an airy shine in a glamorous and versatile elbow-length shawl. The beads are placed one at a time while working, their weight enhancing the shawl's rich drape.

### KNITTED MEASUREMENTS
**Width (end to end)** Approx 76"/193cm
**Length (at center)** Approx 20"/51cm

### MATERIALS
• 4 .88oz/25g balls (each approx 191yd/175m) of **Zealana** Air (cashmere/possum/silk) in #A15 Grey
• One size 5 (3.75mm) circular needle, 40"/100cm long, OR SIZE TO OBTAIN GAUGE
• One size 15 (0.50mm) steel crochet hook
• Stitch markers
• Stitch holders
• 1900 size 8 seed beads in #40 Mink from debbieabrahams.com

### GAUGE
19 sts and 32 rows to 4"/10cm over chart pats using size 5 (3.75mm) needle.
TAKE TIME TO CHECK GAUGE.

### NOTES
**1)** Charts show RS rows only. On all WS rows, sl 1 wyif, k1, p to last 2 sts, k2.
**2)** Circular needle is used to accommodate the large number of sts. Do not join.

### STITCH GLOSSARY
**place 1 bead** With crochet hook, place bead onto next st on LH needle, then knit the st.

### LACE BIND-OFF
K2, sl both sts back to LH needle, k2tog tbl, *k1, sl both sts on RH needle back to LH needle, k2tog tbl; rep from * to end, fasten off last st.

### SHAWL
Tab
Cast on 3 sts.
**Row 1** Sl 1, k2.
**Row 2** Sl 1 wyif, p2.
Rep last 2 rows twice more.

Set-up Rows
**Row 1 (RS)** Sl 1, k2, rotate and pick up and k 3 sts along side edge of tab, rotate and pick up and k 3 from cast-on edge—9 sts.
**Row 2 and all WS rows** Sl 1 wyif, k1, p to last 2 sts, k2.
**Row 3** Sl 1 wyif, k1, [yo, k1] 5 times, yo, k2—15 sts.
**Row 5** Sl 1 wyif, [k1, yo] 3 times, k to last 4 sts, [yo, k1] twice, yo, k2—21 sts.
**Row 6** Rep row 2.

Begin Chart 1
**Row 1 (RS)** Work to rep line, work 12-st rep once, work to end of chart.
Cont to work chart in this way through row 24—93 sts.
Work rows 1–24 of chart 1 three times more, working 6 additional reps of 12-st rep each time—309 sts.

Begin Chart 2
**Row 1 (RS)** Work to rep line, work 12-st rep 25 times, work to end of chart.
Cont to work chart in this way through row 24—381 sts.
Work rows 1–24 of chart 2 once more, working 6 additional reps of 12-st rep—453 sts.

Begin Chart 3
**Row 1 (RS)** Work to rep line, work 12-st rep
37 times, work to end of chart.
Cont to work chart in this way through row
12—489 sts.
Bind off using lace bind-off.

FINISHING
Weave in ends. Block and pin to
measurements. •

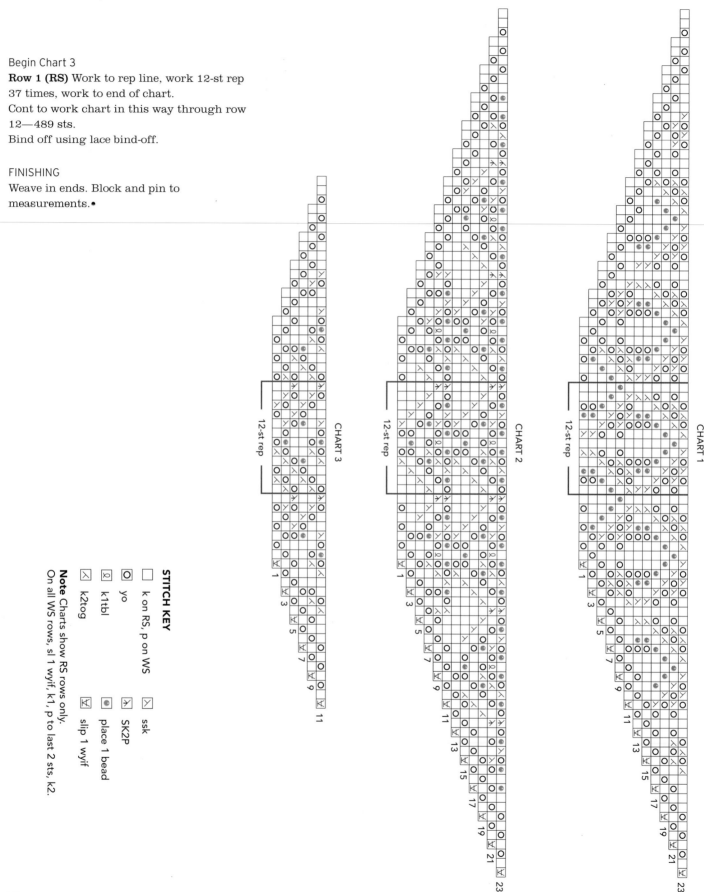

CHART 3

CHART 2

CHART 1

12-st rep

**STITCH KEY**

| | | | |
|---|---|---|---|
| ☐ | k on RS, p on WS | | |
| O | yo | ⋋ | ssk |
| Ω | k1tbl | ⋌ | SK2P |
| ◉ | place 1 bead | | |
| ⋋ | k2tog | ⅄ | slip 1 wyif |

**Note** Charts show RS rows only.
On all WS rows, sl 1 wyif, k1, p to last 2 sts, k2.

# LEAF LACE WRAP

Yoko Hatta's allover leafy lace pattern will become second nature as a series of yarnovers and decreases are worked on both sides of this capacious rectangular wrap. Large enough for wraparound warmth yet light enough to drape around your neck, don't underestimate this beauty's versatility.

### KNITTED MEASUREMENTS
Approx 18 x 60"/45.5 x 152.5cm

### MATERIALS
• 3  3½oz/100g hanks (each approx 437yd/400m) of **Cascade Yarns** Heritage Silk (wool/silk) in #5617 Raspberry (**1**)
• One pair size 4 (3.5mm) needles, OR SIZE TO OBTAIN GAUGE

### GAUGE
28 sts and 36 rows to 4"/10cm over chart using size 4 (3.5mm) needles.
TAKE TIME TO CHECK GAUGE.

### NOTE
Chart rep is inc'd to 18 sts every RS row and dec'd to 17 sts every WS row.

### WRAP
Cast on 128 sts. Knit 4 rows.
**Next row (WS)** P2, k1, p3, k1, [p12, k1, p3, k1] 7 times, p2.

### Begin Chart
**Row 1 (RS)** Work to rep line, work 17-st rep 7 times, work to end of chart.
Cont to work chart in this way through row 16, then rep rows 1–16 for 32 times more.
Knit 3 rows. Bind off.

### FINISHING
Weave in ends. Block to measurements. •

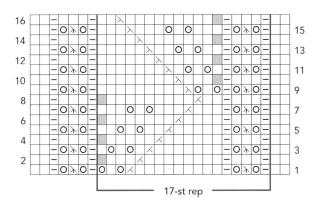

17-st rep

### STITCH KEY

☐ k on RS, p on WS

─ p on RS, k on WS

⟋ k2tog on RS, p2tog on WS

⟍ ssk on RS, p2tog tbl on WS

○ yo

⋏ SK2P

▨ no stitch

# LIGHTWEIGHT PULLOVER

Zahra Jade Knott's sprightly short-sleeved pullover is full of surprises: six distinctive eyelet patterns of polka dots and stripes. A standard fit and gentle V-neck complete a look that is perfect for those in-between seasons.

■■■■▬

### SIZES
Small/Medium (Large, X-Large).
Shown in size Small/Medium.

### KNITTED MEASUREMENTS
**Bust** 39 (42, 45)"/99 (106.5, 114)cm
**Length** 24¾ (25¼, 26¼)"/63 (64, 66.5)cm
**Upper arm** 13 (14, 16)"/33 (35.5, 40.5)cm

### MATERIALS
• 2 (2, 3) 3½oz/100g skeins (each approx 860yd/785m) of **Ancient Arts Fibre Crafts** Lace Weight (superwash wool) in #GM01 Gold Mine (**1**)
• One pair size 3 (3.25mm) needles, OR SIZE TO OBTAIN GAUGES
• Stitch markers

### GAUGES
• 32 sts and 40 rows to 4"/10cm over St st using size 3 (3.25mm) needles.
• 33 sts and 44 rows to 4"/10cm over eyelet pats, after blocking, using size 3 (3.25mm) needles.
TAKE TIME TO CHECK GAUGES.

### SLOPED BIND-OFF
**1)** *One row before the next bind-off row, work to the last st of the row. Do not work this st. Turn work.
**2)** Wyib, sl first st from left needle purlwise.
**3)** Pass unworked st of previous row over the slipped st. The first st is bound off. Cont to bind off desired number of sts for that row. Work to end of row. Rep from* until bind-off is complete.

### PURL RIDGE STRIPE
(over any number of sts)
**Row 1 (RS)** Knit.
**Row 2** Knit.
**Row 3** Purl.
**Rows 4 and 5** Rep rows 2 and 3.
**Row 6** Purl.
These 6 rows form the purl ridge stripe.

### EYELET PATTERN 1
(multiple of 3 sts plus 6)
**Row 1 (RS)** K3, *yo, sl 1, k2, pass the sl st over the k2; rep from * to last 3 sts, k3.
**Row 2 and all WS rows** Purl.
**Row 3** K5, *yo, sl 1, k2, pass the sl st over the k2; rep from * to last 4 sts, k4.
**Row 5** K4, *yo, sl 1, k2, pass the sl st over the k2; rep from * to last 5 sts, k5.
**Row 6** Purl.
**Rows 7–12** Rep rows 1–6.
These 12 rows form eyelet pat 1.

### EYELET PATTERNS 2, 3, 4, AND 6
See charts.

### EYELET PATTERN 5
(multiple of 3 sts plus 6)
**Row 1 (RS)** K3, *yo, sl 1, k2, pass the sl st over the k2; rep from * to last 3 sts, k3.
**Row 2** Purl.
**Row 3** Knit.

**Row 4** Purl.
**Rows 5–8** Rep rows 1–4 once.
**Rows 9 and 10** Rep rows 1 and 2.
These 10 rows form eyelet pat 5.

## BACK

Cast on 162 (174, 186) sts. Beg with a RS row, work in St st
(k on RS, p on WS) for 4 rows.
**Row 1 (RS)** K2, *p2, k2; rep from * to end.
**Row 2** P2, *k2, p2; rep from * to end.
Rep rows 1 and 2 for k2, p2 rib twice more.

### Begin Eyelet Pattern Bands

*Work 6 rows of purl ridge stripe.
Work 12 rows of eyelet pat 1.
Work 6 rows of purl ridge stripe.
Work eyelet pat 2 chart as foll: Work first 11 sts of chart, work
4-st rep 37 (40, 43) times, work last 3 sts of chart. Cont in this
way through chart row 10.
Work 6 rows of purl ridge stripe.
Work eyelet pat 3 chart as foll: Work first 3 sts of chart, work
8-st rep 19 (21, 22) times, work sts 12–18 (16–18, 12–18). Cont
in this way through chart row 10.
Work 6 rows of purl ridge stripe.
Work eyelet pat 4 chart as foll: Beg with st 1 (3, 1), work to
rep, work 4-st rep 37 (41, 43) times, work sts 12–18 (12–16,
12–18). Cont in this way through chart row 10.
Work 6 rows of purl ridge stripe.
Work 10 rows of eyelet pat 5.
Work 6 rows of purl ridge stripe.
Work eyelet pat 6 chart as foll: Work first 3 sts of chart, work
8-st rep 19 (21, 22) times, work sts 12–18 (16–18, 12–18). Cont
in this way through chart row 10.*
Rep between *s (98 rows) to end of piece, AT THE SAME TIME,
work until piece measures 17"/43cm from beg—there should be
12 purl ridge stripes completed plus rows 1 and 2 of eyelet pat 6.

### Armhole Shaping

Bind off 4 (5, 6) sts at beg of next 2 rows.
**Dec row (RS)** K3, ssk, work pat to the last 5 sts, k2tog, k3.
**Next row** P4, work pat to the last 4 sts, p4.
Rep the last 2 rows 7 (8, 9) times more—138 (146, 154) sts.
Work even until armhole measures 6 (6½, 7½)"/15 (16.5, 19)cm.
**Inc row (RS)** K4, M1 in pat, work to last 4 sts, M1 in pat, k4.
Rep inc row every 4th row once more—142 (150, 158) sts.
Work even until the armhole measures 6¾ (7¼, 8¼)"/17 (18.5,
21)cm, place marker each side of the center 40 (44, 46) sts on
last WS row.

### Shoulder Shaping

Using sloped bind-off method, bind off 10 (8, 11) sts at beg of
next 2 rows, then 9 (10, 10) sts from each shoulder edge 4 times,
AT THE SAME TIME, on the first bind-off row, bind off center
40 (44, 46) sts between markers and working both sides at once,
dec 1 st each side of neck edge every other row 5 times.

## FRONT

Work as for back until 12 purl ridge stripes are completed and
piece measures approx 16¾"/42.5cm from beg.

### Left Neck Shaping

**Note** Armhole shaping will take place (as on the back)
simultaneously with the neck shaping after 2 more rows have
been worked.
**Next row (RS)** Work 81 (87, 93) sts, turn, leaving the right
neck sts on hold.
**Next row (WS)** Bind off 2 sts, work to end.
Cont to shape neck, binding off 2 sts at neck edge 3 (4, 4) times
more. Then cont with the armhole shaping, work neck dec row
on RS rows as foll:
**Dec row (RS)** Work to last 3 sts, k2tog, k1.
Rep dec row every other row 9 (9, 10) times more, then every
4th row 7 times—46 (48, 51) sts rem after all armhole dec/inc
shaping.
Work even until armhole measures same as back.

### Shoulder Shaping

Bind off 10 (8, 11) sts from armhole edge once, 9 (10, 10) sts
4 times.

### Right Neck Shaping

Rejoin yarn at center neck edge, bind off 2 sts and work to end.
Cont to work the armhole shaping as on the left side, AT THE
SAME TIME, bind off 2 sts at neck edge 3 (4, 4) times more.
**Dec row (RS)** K1, ssk, work to end.
Rep dec row every other row 9 (9, 10) times more, then every
4th row 7 times.
Complete as for left side.

## SLEEVES

Cast on 92 (100, 116) sts. Work in St st for 4 rows.
Work in k2, p2 rib for 6 rows.
Work 6 rows of purl ridge stripe.
Then cont in St st only, inc 1 st each side of next row and rep
inc every 6th row 5 times more—104 (112, 128) sts.
Work even until piece measures 4½"/11.5cm from beg.

Cap Shaping

Using sloped bind-off, bind off 4 (5, 6) sts at beg of next 2 rows, 3 sts at beg of next 2 rows. Bind off 2 sts at beg of next 26 rows. Bind off rem 38 (44, 58) sts.

FINISHING

Block pieces to measurements. Sew right shoulder seam.

Neckband

With RS facing, pick up and k 56 (60, 66) sts along left neck edge, pm, 1 st at center V-neck, 56 (60, 66) sts along right neck edge, and 60 (64, 66) sts from back neck edge—173 (185, 199) sts.

**Row 1 (WS)** Purl.

Work rows 2–6 of purl ridge stripe, 6 rows of k2, p2 rib, AT THE SAME TIME, dec 1 st each side of center st every RS row as foll:

**Dec row (RS)** Work to 1 st before center st, place new marker, S2KP (removing old marker), work to end.

After last rib row is completed, work as foll:

**Next row (RS)** K to 1 st before center marked st, M1, k1, M1, k to end.

Purl 1 row.

Rep last 2 rows once more. Bind off.

Sew other shoulder and neckband seam. Set in sleeves. Sew side and sleeve seams. Weave in ends. Steam-block finished garment, if necessary.•

## EYELET PATTERN 2

## EYELET PATTERN 3

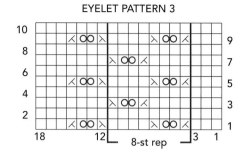

## EYELET PATTERN 4

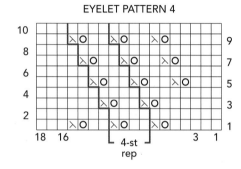

## EYELET PATTERN 6

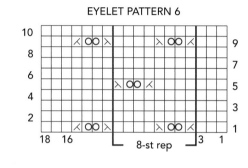

**STITCH KEY**

☐ k on RS, p on WS

◺ k2tog

◹ ssk

◯ yo

◯◯ yo twice*

*p into front and back
of double yo on WS row

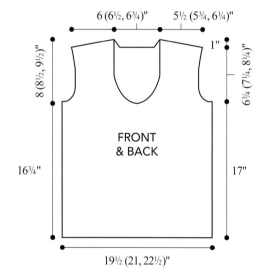

FRONT
& BACK

6 (6½, 6¾)"   5½ (5¾, 6¼)"

8 (8½, 9½)"

1"

6¾ (7¼, 8¼)"

16¾"

17"

19½ (21, 22½)"

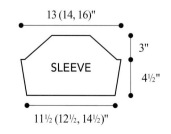

SLEEVE

13 (14, 16)"

3"

4½"

11½ (12½, 14½)"

# FINE MESH PULLOVER

Kristina McGowan's casually sophisticated top is destined to become a wardrobe essential. Knit flat in an allover mesh pattern from the wide scoop-neck collar down, the piece separates for raglan sleeves, front, and back. Deep ribbed cuffs give an extra accentuation to the graceful blouson sleeves.

### SIZES
Small (Medium, Large, X-Large).
Shown in size Small.

### KNITTED MEASUREMENTS
**Bust** 35 ½ (39, 43, 46)"/90 (99, 109, 117)cm
**Length** 21¾ (23, 24, 25)"/55 (58.5, 61, 63.5)cm
**Upper arm** 12 ½ (13, 13¼, 13¾)"/32 (33, 34, 35)cm

### MATERIALS
• Original Yarn
6 (7, 8, 9) 1¾oz/50g balls (each approx 179yd/164m) of **Schulana/Skacel Collection, Inc.** Seda-Mar (silk/nylon) in #01 White ( 2 )
• Substitute Yarn
5 (6, 7, 8) 1¾oz/50g balls (each approx 240yd/220m) in (silk/cotton/nylon) of **Berroco** Summer Silk in #4001 Surf ( 2 )
• One size 6 (4mm) circular needle, 24"/60cm long, OR SIZE TO OBTAIN GAUGE
• One size G-6 (4mm) crochet hook
• Stitch markers
• Stitch holder

### GAUGE
18 sts and 40 rows to 4"/10cm over mesh pat (unstretched) using size 6 (4mm) needle.
TAKE TIME TO CHECK GAUGE.

### NOTE
Pullover is worked from the top down. Ribbed collar is worked in the round, then yoke is worked back and forth in rows. Front, back, and sleeves are worked separately back and forth in rows.

### MESH PATTERN
(multiple of 2 sts)
**Row 1** K1, *yo, p2tog; rep from * to last st, k1.
Rep row 1 for mesh pat.

### YOKE
Cast on 152 sts. Join, taking care not to twist sts, and pm for beg of rnd.
**Rnd 1** *K1, p1; rep from * around.
Rep rnd 1 for k1, p1 rib for 1"/2.5cm.

ROSE CALLAHAN

**Note** Yoke is now worked back and forth in rows. Slip markers every row.

**Row 1 (RS)** K1, pm, work 56 sts in mesh pat for back, pm, k1, pm, work 18 sts in mesh pat for left sleeve, pm, k1, pm, work 56 sts in mesh pat for front, pm, k1, pm, work 18 sts in mesh pat for right sleeve.

**Row 2 (WS)** [Work mesh pat to marker, p1] 4 times.

Cont in this way for 2 (6, 6, 6) rows more.

**Next (inc) row (RS)** [K1, (k1, yo, k1) in same st, work mesh pat to 1 st before marker, (k1, yo, k1) in same st] 4 times—16 sts inc'd.

Rep inc row every 4th (0, 0, 0, 0) rows 1 (0, 0, 0, 0) time, then every 12th (8th, 8th, 8th) row 4 (7, 9, 11) times, working inc'd sts into pat—248 (280, 312, 344) sts.

Work 1 row.

Rep inc row every 2nd (4th, 2nd, 0) row for sleeve sections only 3 (2, 1, 0) times—272 (296, 320, 344) sts, 80 (88, 96, 104) for front and back, 54 (58, 62, 66) for each sleeve, and 1 st at each of 4 seams.

Work 1 (3, 3, 0) rows even.

With crochet hook, slip stitch raglan seam to join yoke. Place sts for back and sleeves (including seam sts) on st holder.

## FRONT

Cast on 1 st at beg of next 2 rows—82 (90, 98, 106) sts.

Cont in mesh pat until front measures 13"/33cm from underarm, end with a WS row.

**Next row (RS)** Purl.

**Next row** *K1, p1; rep from * to end.

Rep last row for k1, p1 rib for 1"/2.5cm.

Bind off loosely.

## BACK

Place 80 (88, 96, 104) sts on hold for back on needle.

Complete as for front.

## SLEEVES

**Note** Knit seam sts every row.

Place sleeve sts and 1 seam st each side on needle—56 (60, 64, 68) sts.

Work in mesh pat as established until sleeve measures 4"/10cm from underarm, end with a WS row.

Dec 0 (1, 1, 1) st each side on next row, then every 0 (0, 60th, 40th) row 0 (0, 1, 2) times more—56 (58, 60, 62) sts.

Work even until sleeve measures 16 (16, 16½, 16½)"/40.5 (40.5, 42, 42)cm from underarm, end with a WS row.

**Next row (RS)** Purl, dec'ing 14 sts evenly across—42 (44, 46, 48) sts.

**Next row** *K1, p1; rep from * to end.

Rep last row for k1, p1 rib for 4"/10cm.

Bind off loosely.

## FINISHING

Sew side and sleeve seams. Weave in ends.•

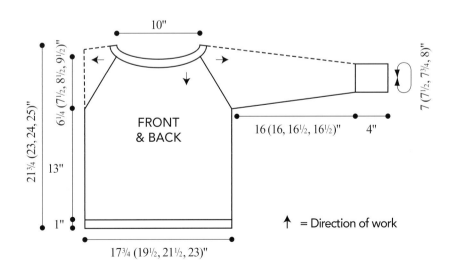

# WAVE LACE SCARF

Wei Wilkins magically transforms a simple repeating pattern of decreases and yarnovers into a sea of eyelet waves. Equally suited wrapped atop a winter coat or draped casually around the neck as an all-day accessory, this scarf adds the perfect touch of warmth and fashion for any occasion.

### KNITTED MEASUREMENTS
**Width** 8"/20.5cm
**Length** 65"/165cm

### MATERIALS
• 2  1¾oz/50g hanks (each approx 170yd/155m) of **Manos del Uruguay** Serena (baby alpaca/cotton) in #2318 Glacier (2)
• One pair each size 4 and 6 (3.5 and 4mm) needles, OR SIZE TO OBTAIN GAUGE
• Stitch markers
• Stitch holder

### GAUGE
26 sts and 30 rows to 4"/10cm over chart using smaller needles.
TAKE TIME TO CHECK GAUGE.

### NOTE
Every RS row, each 8-st rep increases 1 st. Every WS row, each rep decreases back to 8 sts.

### SCARF
With larger needles, cast on 52 sts.
Change to smaller needles. Purl 1 row.

### Begin Chart
**Row 1 (RS)** K2 (selvage sts), work 8-st rep 6 times, k2 (selvage sts).
Cont to work chart in this way, working selvage sts in St st (k on RS, p on WS), through row 12, then rep rows 1–12 until piece measures approx 65"/165cm, end with a row 6. With larger needle, bind off in k1, p1 rib.

### FINISHING
Weave in ends. Block lightly to measurements.•

### STITCH KEY
☐ k on RS, p on WS

◩ k2tog on RS, p2tog on WS

◪ ssk on RS, p2tog tbl on WS

○ yo

▨ no stitch

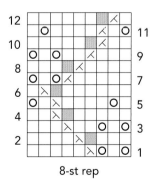

8-st rep

PAUL AMATO

# SIDEWAYS COWL

Change your perspective with Carol J. Sulcoski's easygoing cowl. It's knit in the round in one sleek piece, and the lace at hand is of botanical inspiration with leafy strips separated by swaths of garter stitch enclosed on each side with bands of stockinette.

■■■▭

KNITTED MEASUREMENTS
**Circumference** 28¼"/71.5cm
**Length** 12½"/31.5cm

MATERIALS
• 2  1¾oz/50g balls (each approx 328yd/300m) of **Lotus Yarns/Trendsetter Yarn Group** Mimi (mink) in #10 Green
• One size 4 (3.5mm) circular needle, 24"/60cm long, OR SIZE TO OBTAIN GAUGE
• Stitch marker

GAUGE
24 sts and 35 rnds to 4"/10cm over lace pat, after blocking, using size 4 (3.5mm) needle.
TAKE TIME TO CHECK GAUGE.

NOTE
Stitch count changes throughout lace pattern.

COWL
Cast on 170 sts. Join, taking care not to twist sts, and pm for beg of rnd.
Work in garter st (k 1 rnd, p 1 rnd) for 6 rnds.

Begin Lace Pattern
**Rnd 1 and all odd rnds** Knit.
**Inc rnd 2** *P5, k5, ssk, yo, k5, [yo, k1] 5 times, yo, k5, yo, k2tog, k5; rep from * around—200 sts.
**Rnd 4** *P5, k5, ssk, yo, ssk, k1, [k2tog, yo] twice, k3, yo, k1, yo, k3, [yo, ssk] twice, k1, k2tog, yo, k2tog, k5; rep from * around.
**Rnd 6** *P5, k5, ssk, yo, S2KP, yo, k2tog, yo, k5, yo, k1, yo, k5, yo, ssk, yo, S2KP, yo, k2tog, k5; rep from * around.
**Dec rnd 8** *P5, k5, SK2P, yo, k2tog, yo, k1, yo, ssk, k1, k2tog, yo, S2KP, yo, ssk, k1, k2tog, yo, k1, yo, ssk, yo, k3tog, k5; rep from * around—180 sts.
**Dec rnd 10** *P5, k6, k2tog, yo, k3, [yo, S2KP] 3 times, yo, k3, yo, ssk, k6; rep from * around—170 sts.
Rep rnds 1–10 nine times more.
Work in garter st for 6 rnds. Bind off.

FINISHING
Weave in ends. Block to measurements.●

# MEDALLION WEDDING DRESS

Nicky Epstein pulled out all the stops in celebration of *Vogue Knitting*'s 30th anniversary with a stunning two-piece wedding gown that is all about pearlescent beauty. The shaped top is worked from side to side with a sprinkling of pearls across the bodice and a dramatically scooped back, and the skirt is made up of medallions worked in the round. Perfect dress, perfect day.

■■■■

### SIZES
Small/Medium (Large/X-Large). Shown in size Small/Medium.

### KNITTED MEASUREMENTS
**Bust** 36 (40)"/91.5 (101.5)cm
**Length of top** 22 (23)"/56 (58.5)cm
**Waist (closed)** 24 (30)"/61 (76)cm
**Hip (where joined to top)** 33 (38½)"/83.5 (97.5)cm
**Length of skirt (waistband to lowest point of dip)** 40"/101.5cm

### MATERIALS
• 3 (4) .88oz/25g hanks (each approx 312yd/285m) of **Artyarns** Silk Mohair Glitter (mohair/silk with metallic) in #250 Silver Cream (A) (1)
• 3 (4) 1¾oz/50g hanks (each approx 110yd/101m of **Artyarns** Beaded Silk & Sequins Light (silk with glass beads) in #250 Silver Cream (B) (3)
• 2 (3) hanks in #167 silver beige and pink multi (C)
• 2 (3) 2¾oz/80g hanks each (each approx 400yd/366m) **Artyarns** Ensemble Glitter Light (cashmere/silk with metallic) in #250 silver cream (D) and #257 silver beige (E) (3)
• One pair size 5 (3.75mm) needles, OR SIZE TO OBTAIN GAUGES
• One size 5 (3.75mm) circular needle, 24"/60cm long
• One set (4) size 5 (3.75mm) double-pointed needles (dpn)
• One size F-5 (3.75mm) crochet hook
• 30 8mm imitation Crystallized Swarovski Elements Crystal Pearls in #001 620 crystal cream pearl
• 68"/172.5cm satin ribbon for belt
• One ⅞"/22mm snap
• 1yd/1m ½"/1.5cm elastic for waistband
• Stitch marker
• Sewing needle and thread

### GAUGES
• 20 sts and 38 rows to 4"/10cm over stripe pat using 2 strands of A held tog and B and size 5 (3.75mm) needles.
• 20 sts and 30 rows to 4"/10cm over St st using E and size 5 (3.75mm) needles.
• One circle is approx 7½"/19cm in diameter.
TAKE TIME TO CHECK GAUGES.

### NOTES
**1)** A is used with 2 strands held tog throughout.
**2)** When working stripe pat, carry color not in use up the side of work.

(over any number of sts)
**Row 1 (RS)** With 2 strands of A held tog, knit.
**Row 2** Purl.
**Short-row 3** K to last 20 sts, w&t.
**Short-row 4** Purl.
**Rows 5 and 6** Rep rows 1 and 2.
**Row 7** With B, purl.
**Row 8** With B, knit.
**Rows 9 and 10** Rep rows 7 and 8.
Rep rows 1–10 for stripe pat.

SKIRT

Waist

With E, cast on 166 (192) sts. Work in St st (k on RS, p on WS) for 1"/2.5cm, end with a WS row.
**Next (turning ridge) row (RS)** Purl.
Cont in St st until piece measures 6"/15cm from turning ridge. Bind off.
Fold to WS along turning ridge and sew to form waistband casing, leaving ends open. Run elastic through casing and cut elastic to fit. Sew each end of casing to secure elastic.

Circles

(make 17 (22) in D & C; 3 in D & B; 13 in E & B)
With dpn and D (D, E) cast on 10 sts and divide over 3 dpn as foll: 4 sts, 2 sts, 4 sts. Join, taking care not to twist sts, and pm for beg of rnd.

Begin Chart

**Rnd 1** Work chart row 1, rep 5 times around—15 sts.
Cont to foll chart in this manner until rnd 22 is complete—25 sts in each rep, 125 sts in rnd.
With C (B, B), purl 3 rnds. Bind off.

Skirt Finishing

Foll diagram (see page 90), lay circles on a flat surface and pin tog where indicated by double green lines. Arrange to obtain the desired shape. For smaller size, omit red circles.
**Note** In order to create dip in lower edge, each circle is joined to others in a different number of places.
When circles are pinned, sew tog with seams approx 2–3½"/5–9cm long.
Once circles are sewn tog, but not joined at back into round, sew top row of 5 (6) circles to skirt waist, with tops of circles overlapping lower edge of skirt waist approx 2"/5cm.
Sew center back seam of skirt waist, sew circles into round at center back foll diagram. Sew snap to waistband, allowing an overlap of 1"/2.5cm.

## TOP

### Front Bodice

With straight needles and 2 strands of A held tog, cast on 60 (62) sts.

Work rows 5–10 of stripe pat, then work rows 1–6.

**Inc row 7 (RS)** With B, cast on 40 (43) sts, p to end—100 (105) sts.

Cont in stripe pat as established until row 10 is complete.

Rep rows 1–10 for 4 (5) times more.

### Left front neck shaping

**Next row (RS)** With A, bind off 14 sts.

Cont in pat, dec 1 st at neck edge every other row twice—84 (89) sts.

Cont in pat until row 10 has been worked 5 times more.

Rep rows 1 and 2 once more.

### Right front neck shaping

Cont in pat and inc 1 st at neck edge every other row twice—86 (91) sts.

**Row 6 (WS)** P to end, cast on 14 sts—100 (105) sts.

Cont in pat until row 10 has been worked 5 (6) times more.

**Next row (RS)** With B, bind off 40 (43) sts—60 (62) sts.

Change to A and cont in pat until row 10 has been worked once more. With A, rep rows 5 and 6 once more. Bind off.

### Back

Work same as for front to left front neck shaping.

### Right back neck shaping

**Next row (RS)** With A, bind off 50 sts, work to end.

Cont in pat and bind off 3 sts from neck edge once, then dec 1 st every other row 3 times—44 (49) sts.

Cont in pat until row 10 has been worked 4 times more.

Work rows 1–8 once more.

### Left back neck shaping

Inc 1 st at neck edge every other row 3 times, cast on 3 sts at neck edge once—50 (55) sts. Work 1 row even.

**Next row (RS)** With B, cast on 50 sts, cont in pat to end—100 (105) sts.

Work until row 10 has been worked 5 (6) times more.

**Next row (RS)** With B, bind off 40 (43) sts—60 (62) sts.

Change to A and cont in pat until row 10 has been worked once more. With A, rep rows 5 and 6 once more. Bind off.

### Sleeves

Make 2 circles in D and C same as for skirt.

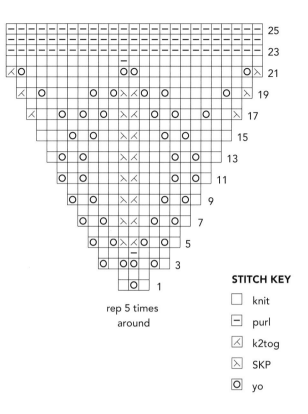

rep 5 times
around

**STITCH KEY**

☐ knit

⊟ purl

◺ k2tog

◿ SKP

◉ yo

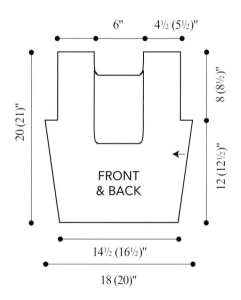

6"     4½ (5½)"

8 (8½)"

20 (21)"

12 (12½)"

FRONT & BACK

14½ (16½)"

18 (20)"

↑ = Direction of work

Top Finishing

Sew shoulder seams. Sew in sleeves by centering top half of circle to shoulder seam and sewing to each side edge of bodice, leaving lower half of circle open. Sew side seams. With crochet hook and A, work sl st (see page 165) along underarm.

Front neck facing

With circular needle, RS facing and A, pick up and k 33 sts evenly along neck edge (side edge of rows). Change to B and work rows 7–10 of stripe pat. Bind off.

Back neck facing

With circular needle, RS facing and A, pick up and k 35 sts along back neck (side edge of rows) and work same as front. With A, tack each end of neck facings to WS.

Bodice border

With A and circular needle, cast on 178 (200) sts. Work border stripe pat as foll:
[With C, work 4 rows rev St st (p on RS, k on WS). With A, work 4 rows St st] twice.
With C work 4 rows rev St st. With A, bind off.
With A, beg at left side seam and sew cast-on edge of bodice border to lower edge of bodice. Sew side seam of border. Sew 24 pearls to bodice front using photos as guide.

BELT

Flowers (make 3-5 in B and C as desired)
Cast on 6 sts.
**Row 1 (RS)** K3, yo, k3—7 sts.
**Row 2 and all WS rows** Knit.
**Row 3** K3, yo, k4—8 sts.
**Row 5** K3, yo, k5—9 sts.
**Row 7** K3, yo, k6—10 sts.
**Row 9** K3, yo, k7—11 sts.
**Row 11** K3, yo, k8—12 sts.
**Row 12** Bind off 6 sts, k to end—6 sts.
Rep rows 1–12 for 4 times more. Bind off rem 6 sts.
Sew cast-on edge to bound-off edge to form flower. Weave yarn in and out of eyelets, pull tightly to cinch and secure. Sew one pearl in center of each flower. Sew flowers to satin ribbon and tie at waist (see photo).•

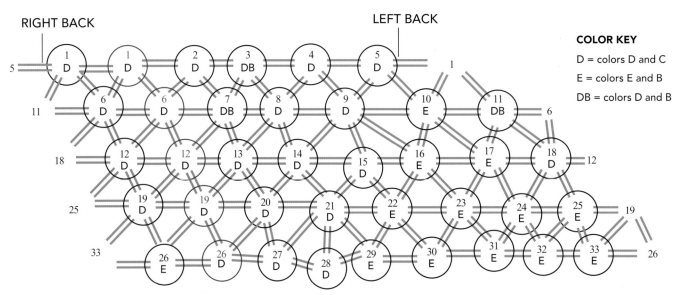

**NOTE** The red circles are for the larger size only. For the smaller size, omit the red circles.

# LACE COAT

Brooke Nico's exquisite, close-fitting lace coat is worked in a variety of openwork patterns. The main body sections are worked multi-directionally off the horizontal bands of the lower edge and waist. Full-fashioned raglan shaping beautifully defines the diamond lace pattern of the bodice, and a gently ruffled section at the lower hem adds flair.

▰▰▰▭

## SIZES
X-Small/Small (Medium).
Shown in size X-Small/Small.

## KNITTED MEASUREMENTS
**Bust** 29½ (35)"/75 (89)cm
**Length** 39 (40)"/99 (101.5)cm
**Upper arm** 13¼ (14½)"/33 (37)cm

## MATERIALS
• Original Yarn
5 (6) 1¾oz/50g balls (each approx 440yd/403m) of **Classic Elite Yarns** Silky Alpaca Lace (alpaca/silk) in #2471 Pixie Pink (**1**)
• Substitute Yarn
5 (6) 1¾oz/50g balls (each approx. 440yd/400m) of **Rowan** Fine Lace (alpaca/wool) in #921 Antique (**1**)
• One each sizes 2 and 5 (2.75mm and 3.75mm) circular needle, each 32"/81cm long, OR SIZE TO OBTAIN GAUGES
• One set (5) each sizes 2 and 5 (2.75mm and 3.75mm) double-pointed needles (dpn)
• Stitch markers
• Stitch holders
• Two ¹³⁄₁₆"/20mm buttons

## GAUGES
• 24 sts and 38 rows/rnds to 4"/10cm over daisy pat (on sleeves and bodice), after blocking, using smaller circular needle.
• 21 sts and 25 rows to 4"/10cm over day lilies pat (on skirt), after blocking, using 2 strands of yarn held tog and larger circular needle.
TAKE TIME TO CHECK GAUGES.

## STITCH GLOSSARY
**4-st decrease** K5, pass 4 sts on RH needle, one at a time, over the first st on RH needle.

## DAY LILIES PATTERN
(beg over multiple of 16 sts plus 5, double stranded)
**Row 1 (RS)** K3, *yo, k2tog, yo, [k2tog] 3 times, k2, yo, k3, yo, ssk, yo, k1; rep from *, end k2.
**Row 2** Purl.
**Row 3** K3, *yo, k2tog, [k3tog] twice, yo, k1, yo, k2, [ssk, yo] twice, k1; rep from *, end k2.
**Row 4** *P12, p2tog; rep from *, end p5.
**Row 5** K3, *yo, k3tog, yo, k3, yo, k2, [ssk, yo] twice, k1; rep from *, end k2.
**Rows 6, 8, and 10** Purl.
**Row 7** K3, *yo, k2tog, yo, k1, yo, k2, ssk, yo, k2, [ssk, yo] twice, k1; rep from *, end k2.
**Row 9** K3, *yo, k2tog, yo, k3, yo, k2, [ssk] 3 times, yo, ssk, yo, k1; rep from *, end k2.
**Row 11** K3, *[yo, k2tog] twice, k2, yo, k1, yo, [SK2P] twice, ssk, yo, k1; rep from *, end k2.
**Row 12** P5, *p2tog tbl, p12; rep from * to end.
**Row 13** K3, *[yo, k2tog] twice, k2, yo, k3, yo, SK2P, yo, k1; rep from *, end k2.
**Row 14** Purl.
**Row 15** K3, *[yo, k2tog] twice, k2, yo, k2tog, k2, yo, k1, yo, ssk, yo, k1; rep from *, end k2.
**Row 16** Purl.
Rep rows 1–16 for day lilies pat.

## COAT
### Border
With 2 strands of yarn held tog and larger circular needle, loosely cast on 30 sts for center front edge of border.
Knit 4 rows.

### Begin charts
Work charts 1, 2, and 3 for hem edging, as foll:
Work rows 1–24 of chart 1 once, rep rows 1–24 of chart 2 for 8 (10) times, and then work rows 1–24 of chart 3 once.

Knit 4 rows. Bind off knitwise, loosely.
Edging measures approx 31½ (37½)"/80 (94)cm along upper straight edge.

## Skirt

With RS facing, work into upper straight edge of border, with 2 strands of yarn and larger needle, pick up and k 165 (197) sts along this edge as foll: 2 sts in first garter border, 16 sts in each of the 10 (12) leaf reps and 3 sts in the final garter border. Purl 1 row on WS.

## Begin Day Lilies Pattern

With 2 strands of yarn and larger needle, work day lilies pat over 10 (12) reps. Work 16-row pat for a total of 6 reps, end with row 14. Skirt measures approx 15"/38cm from border.
**Next row (RS)** K3, *[k2tog] twice, k7, ssk, k1; rep from *, end ssk—114 (136) sts.
**Next row** Bind off 3 sts, p to end.
**Next row (RS)** Bind off 3 sts, then cast on 19 sts to end of needle for the waistband.

## Begin Waistband

**Row 1 (RS)** Work row 1 of chart 1, working only waistband panel sts, k1, then ssk last waistband st tog with 1 st from skirt just worked, turn.
**Row 2** K2, work row 2 of waistband panel to end.
**Note** For size Medium, it will be necessary to work 2 RS waistband rows evenly spaced without joining them to skirt.
Cont to work in this manner, joining waistband to skirt on RS rows until all sts are joined and 24-row rep has been worked for 9 (11) reps. Lay work aside.

## Sleeves

With 2 strands of yarn held tog and larger dpn, cast on 32 (40) sts and divide evenly over 4 needles. Join to work in rnds, taking care not to twist sts, and pm for beg of rnd.
**Rnd 1** Purl.
**Rnd 2** *Yo, k2tog; rep from * around.
**Rnd 3** Knit.
**Rnd 4** *Yo, ssk; rep from * around.
**Rnd 5** Knit.
**Rnd 6** Purl.
Cut 1 strand of yarn and change to smaller dpn. Work with 1 strand only for rem of sleeve.
**Next rnd** K2 (0), *M1, k3 (4); rep from * 9 times more—42 (50) sts.

## Begin daisy pattern

**Inc rnd 1** K1, yo, *k3, yo, ssk, k3; rep from *, end yo, k1.
**Rnd 2 and all even rnds** Knit.
**Rnd 3** *K3, k2tog, yo, k1, yo, ssk; rep from *, end k4.
**Rnd 5** K2, *k2tog, yo, k3, yo, ssk, k1; rep from *, end last rep

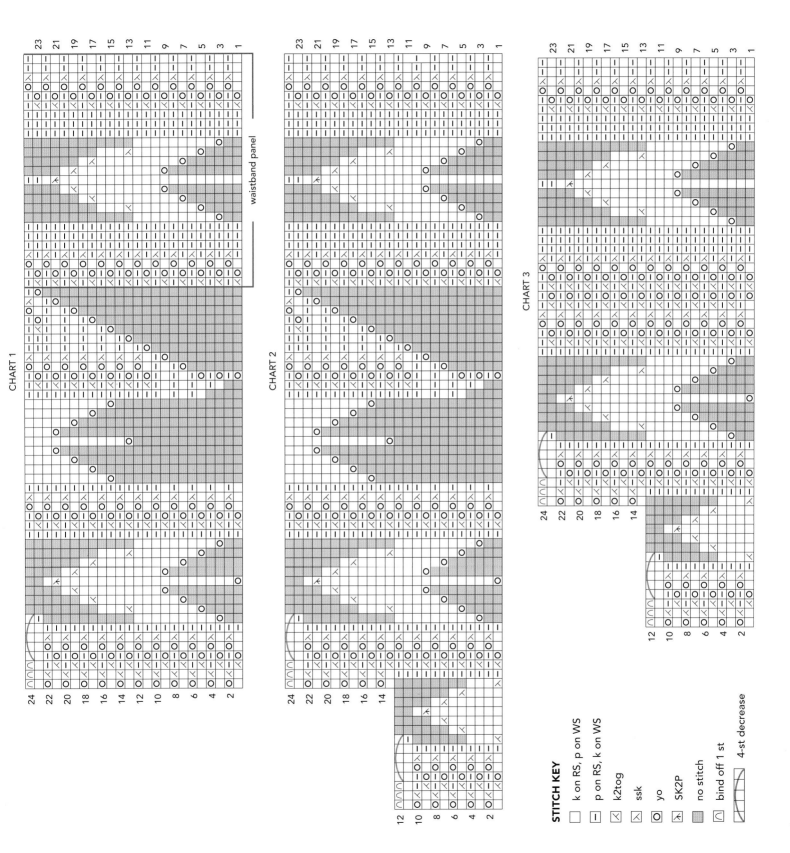

CHART 1

CHART 2

CHART 3

waistband panel

**STITCH KEY**

| | k on RS, p on WS |
| I | p on RS, k on WS |
| ⋉ | k2tog |
| ⋌ | ssk |
| O | yo |
| ⋏ | SK2P |
| | no stitch |
| ∩ | bind off 1 st |
| | 4-st decrease |

k3 instead of k1.

**Inc rnd 7** K1, yo, k3, *yo, SK2P, yo, k5; rep from *, end last rep k4, yo, k1 instead of k5.

**Rnd 9** K2, *yo, ssk, k6; rep from *, end yo, ssk, k2.

**Rnd 11** *K2tog, yo, k1, yo, ssk, k3; rep from *, end last rep k1 instead of k3.

**Inc rnd 13** K1, yo, *k3, yo, ssk, k1, k2tog, yo; rep from *, end k3, yo, k2.

**Rnd 15** K2, *yo, SK2P, yo, k5; rep from *, end last rep k3 instead of k5.

**Rnd 17** K7, *yo, ssk, k6; rep from *, end k1.

**Inc rnd 19** K1, yo, k4, *k2tog, yo, k1, yo, ssk, k3; rep from *, end k1, yo, k2.

**Rnd 21** K2, *yo, ssk, k1, k2tog, yo, k3; rep from * around.

**Rnd 23** K2tog, yo, *k5, yo, SK2P, yo; rep from *, end k5, yo, ssk, k1.

**Rnd 24** Knit.

Rep rnds 1–24 for 3 times more, then rep rnds 1–16 once—80 (88) sts.

Cont to work daisy pat as foll:

**Rnd 1** Move beg of rnd marker 1 st to the right by removing marker, sl last st of previous rnd to LH needle and replace marker, then work as foll: ssk, k6, *yo, ssk, k6; rep from *, end yo.

**Rnd 2 and all even rnds** Knit.

**Rnd 3** *Yo, ssk, k3, k2tog, yo, k1; rep from * around.

**Rnd 5** K1, *yo, ssk, k1, k2tog, yo, k3; rep from * around, end last rep k2 instead of k3.

**Rnd 7** Move beg of rnd marker 1 st to the left by removing marker, sl the first st of rnd to RH needle and replace marker, then work as foll: *yo, k5, yo, SK2P; rep from * around.

**Rnd 9** K3, *yo, ssk, k6; rep from * around, end last rep k3 instead of k6.

**Rnd 11** K1, *k2tog, yo, k1, yo, ssk, k3; rep from *, end last rep k2 instead of k3.

**Rnd 13** *K2tog, yo, k3, yo, ssk, k1; rep from * around.

**Rnd 15** K2, *yo, SK2P, yo, k5; rep from * around, end last rep k3 instead of k5.

**Rnd 16** Knit.

Rep rnds 1–15 once more. Cut yarn. Sl the last 8 sts to holder for underarm and lay work aside with 72 (80) sts for each sleeve.

## Bodice

**Note** When shaping in lace pat, work yo's only if you have matching decs and vice versa.

With 1 strand of yarn and smaller circular needle, pick up and k 189 (221) sts in top edge of waistband. Do not join. Purl 1 row on WS.

Begin chart 4

**Row 1 (RS)** Work to rep line, work 8-st rep 21 (25) times across, work to end of chart—187 (219) sts.

Cont to foll chart in this manner until row 31 is complete—177 (209) sts.

**Joining row (WS)** P36 (44), place next 8 sts on holder for underarm, pm, p72 (80) sleeve sts, pm, p88 (104), place next 8 sts on holder for underarm, pm, p72 (80) sleeve sts, pm, p37 (45)—305 (353) sts.

Raglan shaping

**Next dec row (RS)** [Work to 3 sts before next marker, k2tog, k1, sm, ssk] 4 times, work to end—8 sts dec'd.

Cont to work pat as established, rep dec row every other row 31 (35) times more, AT THE SAME TIME, cont to dec at neck edge every 30th (12th) row 2 (6) times more—45 (53) neck sts.

**Next row (WS)** Purl, removing markers.

Place sts on holder.

Front Bands

With RS facing, larger needles and 2 strands of yarn held tog, beg at lower edge of right front waistband, pick up and k 56 (60) sts evenly along front edge of waistband and bodice, 45 (53) evenly along neck, and 56 (60) sts evenly along front edge bodice and waistband—157 (173) sts.

**Next row (WS)** Knit.

**Next row** K2, *yo, k2tog; rep from * to last st, k1.

Knit 2 rows. Bind off loosely.

## FINISHING

Graft underarm sts. Sew ends of front bands to bound-off sts of upper edge of skirt. Sew buttons to waistband using photo as guide. Weave in ends.•

CHART 4

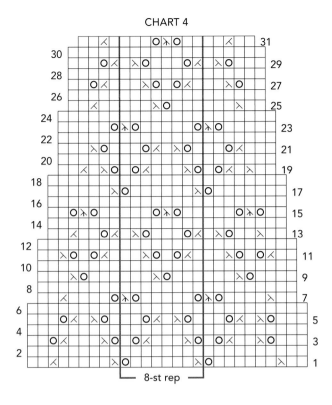

**STITCH KEY**

☐ k on RS, p on WS

◱ k2tog

◲ ssk

⊙ yo

⟰ SK2P

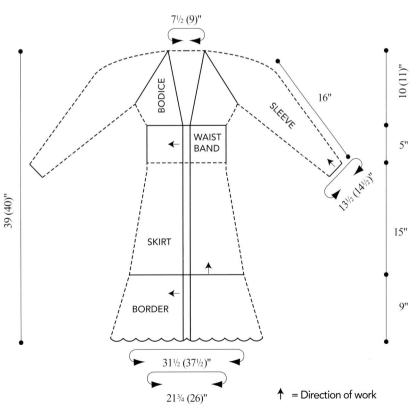

↑ = Direction of work

# DIAMOND & LEAF PONCHO

Traditional triangle shawl shaping is worked on either side of the central lace pattern of Lisa Daehlin's dramatic poncho, which is etched with spectacular swirled lace. The fold-over collar is picked up and knit in a faggoting stitch that's echoed along the lower edge.

■◗■■■◗

## KNITTED MEASUREMENTS
**Circumference (lower edge)** Approx 75"/190.5cm
**Length** Approx 22"/56cm

## MATERIALS
• 10  1¾oz/50g hanks (each approx 175yd/160m) of **Koigu** KPM (wool) in #1101.5 Peach (2)
• Three size 7 (4.5mm) circular needles, each 16, 24, and 40"/40, 60 and 100cm long, OR SIZE TO OBTAIN GAUGE
• Stitch markers

## GAUGE
24 sts and 30 rnds to 4"/10cm over chart 2, after blocking, using size 7 (4.5mm) needle. TAKE TIME TO CHECK GAUGE.

## NOTES
**1)** When working poncho, change to longer circular needles, as necessary.
**2)** When working the collar, the WS is worked on the RS of the poncho so that the RS of collar will show when worn.

## PONCHO
With shortest circular needle, cast on 108 sts as foll:
*Cast on 1 st, pm, cast on 53 sts, pm; rep from * once more. Join, taking care not to twist sts, and pm for beg of rnd.

### Begin Charts 1 and 2
**Rnd 1** [Work rnd 1 of chart 1, sm, work first st of chart 2, work st rep 3 times, work to end of chart 2, sm] twice. Cont to work charts in this manner, and rep rnds 1–16 of chart 2 until rnd 17 of chart 1 is complete—184 sts.
**Next rnd** [Work rnd 10 of chart 1 to rep line, work 18-st rep twice, work to end of chart, work rnd 2 of chart 2] twice—188 sts.
Cont to work charts as established through chart 1 rnd 17 and chart 2 rnd 9—220 sts. Cont to work chart 1 rnds 10–17, working 18-st rep once more for each 8-rnd rep, AT THE SAME TIME, cont chart 2 until 16-rnd rep has been worked 8 times total, end with rnd 16 on both charts 1 and 2—680 sts total, 53 sts each center panel, 287 sts each side section.

### Begin Charts 3 and 4
**Inc rnd 1** [Work chart 3 to rep line, work 22-st rep 15 times, work to end of chart 3, work st rep of chart 4 for 3 times, work to end of chart 4] twice—818 sts.
Cont to work charts in this manner until rnd 4 is complete. Rep rnds 3 and 4 for 9 times more. Bind off in pat.

## FINISHING
### Collar
With WS facing and shortest circular needle, pick up and k 108 sts evenly around neck and pm for beg of rnd.
**Rnd 1** *K2tog, [yo] twice, ssk; rep from * around.
**Rnd 2** K1, (p1, k1) into double yo, k1; rep from * around.
Rep rnds 1 and 2 twelve times more.
**Inc rnd** *Yo, M1, yo, k2tog, [yo] twice, ssk; rep from * around—189 sts.
**Next rnd** *K3, k2tog, [yo] twice, ssk; rep from * around.
**Next rnd** *Yo, SK2P, yo, k2tog, [yo] twice, ssk; rep from * around.
Rep last 2 rnds 8 times. Bind off in pat. Weave in ends. Block to measurements.•

## CHART 1

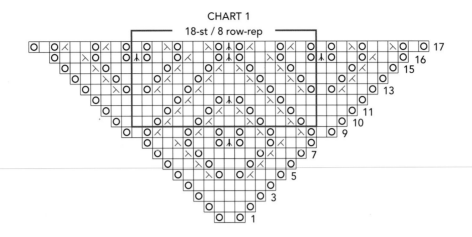

18-st / 8 row-rep

## STITCH KEY

- ☐ k
- ⊟ p
- ⊠ k2tog
- ⊠ ssk
- ⊡ yo
- ⊠ k1 tbl
- ⊼ k3tog
- ⊼ S2KP
- ⊼ SK2P

## CHART 2

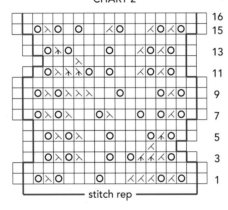

stitch rep

## CHART 3

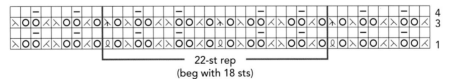

22-st rep
(beg with 18 sts)

## CHART 4

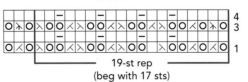

19-st rep
(beg with 17 sts)

# LEAF-TRIMMED SHAWL

Zabeth Loisel Weiner's triangular shawl brings the drama with ravishing openwork that weaves a pattern of waves and open diamonds. This delicate piece is knit from stitches picked up from the undulating lace border and shaped by decreasing by four stitches every right-side row.

■■■■

## KNITTED MEASUREMENTS
**Width (upper edge)** 50"/127cm
**Length** 27"/68.5cm

## MATERIALS
• 1 4oz/114g hank (each approx 840yd/768m) of **Madelinetosh** Prairie (superwash merino wool) in Mourning Dove (**1**)
• One size 6 (4mm) circular needle, 34"/80cm long, OR SIZE TO OBTAIN GAUGE
• Stitch markers

## GAUGE
20 sts and 36 rows to 4"/10cm over St st using size 6 (4mm) needle.
TAKE TIME TO CHECK GAUGE.

## NOTES
**1)** Only RS rows are included in charts, with the exception of row 36 in Chart 1. All WS rows are purled, unless otherwise instructed.
**2)** Circular needle is used to accommodate the large number of sts. Do not join.
**3)** 4 sts are dec'd in each RS row as charts 2–5 are worked.

## STITCH KEY

☐ k on RS, p on WS    ⟋ k2tog    ◯ yo

⊟ p on RS, k on WS    ⟍ ssk    ⊻ sl 1

## STITCH GLOSSARY
**Double yo** Wrap yarn twice around needle. On next row, purl into front and back of yo.

## SHAWL
Border
Cast on 22 sts. Work 6 rows in garter st as foll: Sl 1, k21.

Begin chart 1
**Next row (RS)** Work chart row 1.
**Row 2 and all WS rows** K1, p to end.
Cont to work chart in this manner until row 36 is complete.
Rep rows 1–36 five times more.
Work rows 1–18 and pm for center point of shawl at end of this row.
Work rows 19–36, then rep rows 1–36 six times more—13 reps of chart 1 are complete.
Work 5 rows in garter st as foll: Sl 1, k to end.
Bind off knitwise on WS.

CHART 1

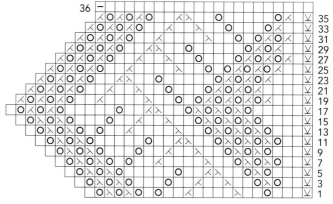

Beg with 22 sts
**Note** Except row 36, only RS rows appear on chart.

## CHART 5 – LEFT HALF

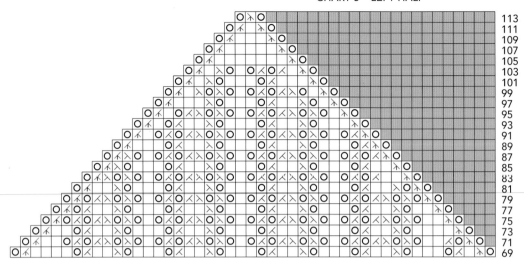

113
111
109
107
105
103
101
99
97
95
93
91
89
87
85
83
81
79
77
75
73
71
69

## CHART 4 - LEFT HALF

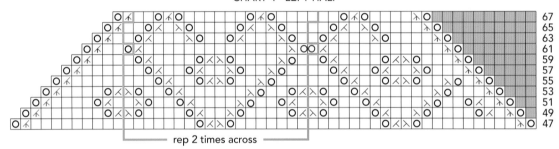

67
65
63
61
59
57
55
53
51
49
47

rep 2 times across

## CHART 3 – LEFT HALF

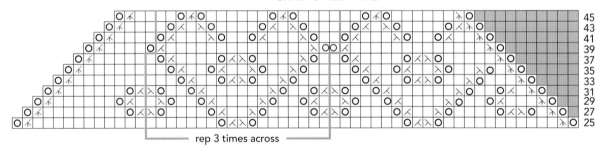

45
43
41
39
37
35
33
31
29
27
25

rep 3 times across

## CHART 2 – LEFT HALF

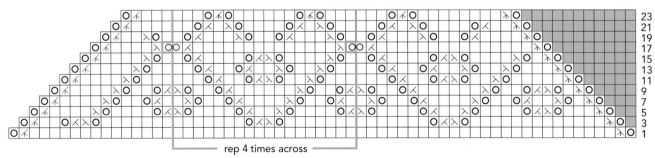

23
21
19
17
15
13
11
9
7
5
3
1

rep 4 times across

104

## CHART 5 – RIGHT HALF

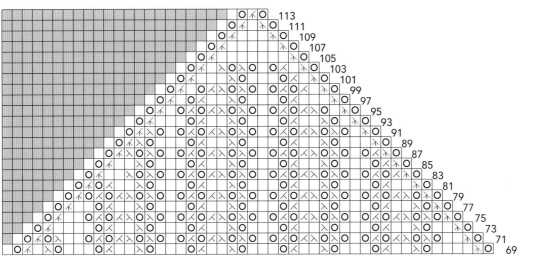

**STITCH KEY**

| | |
|---|---|
| ☐ | k on RS, p on WS |
| ◹ | k2tog |
| ◺ | ssk |
| ◉ | yo |
| ⬈ | SK2P |
| ◸ | k3tog |
| ◉◉ | double yo |
| ▨ | no stitch |

**Note** Only RS rows appear
on charts 2–5. Purl all WS rows
unless otherwise instructed.

## CHART 4 - RIGHT HALF

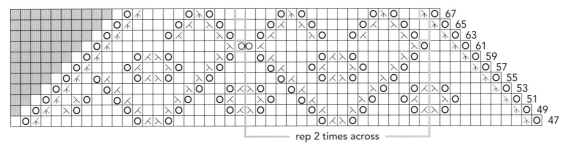

rep 2 times across

## CHART 3 – RIGHT HALF

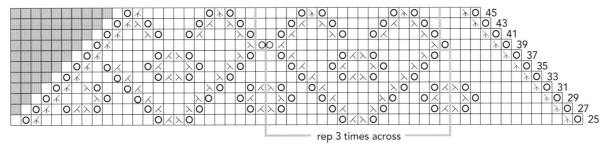

rep 3 times across

## CHART 2 – RIGHT HALF

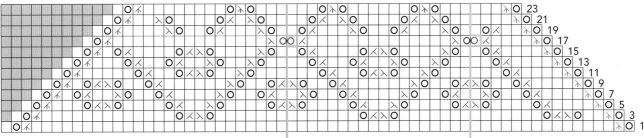

rep 4 times across

Body

With WS of border facing, pick up and k 3 sts along edge of garter st border, 117 sts evenly to center marked st, 1 st for center st, 117 sts evenly to garter st border, and 3 sts in garter st border—241 sts.

Begin chart 2

**Row 1 (RS)** K3, work to rep line, work 18-st rep 4 times across, work to next rep line, work 18-st rep 4 times across, work to end of chart row, k3.

**Row 2 and all WS rows** K3, p to last 3 sts, k3.

Cont to work chart in this manner until row 24 is complete—193 sts.

Begin chart 3

**Row 25 (RS)** K3, work to rep line, work 18-st rep 3 times across, work to next rep line, work 18-st rep 3 times across, work to end of chart row, k3.

**Row 26 and all WS rows** K3, p to last 3 sts, k3.

Cont to work chart in this manner until row 46 is complete—149 sts.

Begin chart 4

**Row 47 (RS)** K3, work to rep line, work 18-st rep twice, work to next rep line, work 18-st rep twice, work to end of chart row, k3.

**Row 48 and all WS rows** K3, p to last 3 sts, k3.

Cont to work chart in this manner until row 68 is complete—105 sts.

Begin chart 5

**Row 69 (RS)** K3, work to end of chart row, k3.

**Row 70 and all WS rows** K3, p to last 3 sts, k3.

Cont to work chart in this manner until row 113 is complete—13 sts.

**Dec row 114 (WS)** K3, p2, p2tog, p3, k3—12 sts.

Divide rem sts evenly over 2 needles and graft tog.

FINISHING

Weave in ends. Block to measurements, pinning each point of border.•

# DAINTY LACE FINGERLESS GLOVES

A mock cable interspersed with eyelets and dainty netting are utilized in Linda Medina's short and sweet fingerless gloves. Worked in the round with a ribbed palm and edges, we recommend using the most luxurious yarn in your stash for these intricate accessories.

**KNITTED MEASUREMENTS**
**Circumference** 7½"/19cm
**Length** 6"/15cm

**MATERIALS**
• 1  2oz/55g hanks (each approx 400yd/366m) of **Jade Sapphire Exotic Fibres** Mongolian Cashmere 2-ply (cashmere) in #130 Dorothy's Dress
• One set (4) size 4 (3.5mm) double-pointed needles (dpn), OR SIZE TO OBTAIN GAUGE
• Stitch markers
• Stitch holders

**GAUGE**
26 sts and 37 rows to 4"/10cm over chart pat using size 4 (3.5mm) needles.
TAKE TIME TO CHECK GAUGE.

**LEFT GLOVE**
Cast on 52 sts and divide evenly over dpn. Join, taking care not to twist sts, and pm for beg of rnd. Knit 5 rnds.
**Picot rnd** *K2tog, yo; rep from * around.
Knit 5 rnds.

Begin Chart
**Next rnd** Work rnd 1 of chart across 34 sts, [k1, p1] 9 times for k1, p1 rib across palm sts.
Cont in this way until rnds 1–8 of chart have been completed 4 times, then rep rows 1–6 once more.

ROSE CALLAHAN

Divide for Thumb

Sl 4 sts just worked to st holder for thumb.

**Next rnd** K3, yo, SK2P, sl these 5 sts to thumb st holder, beg
with stitch 6, work chart rnd 7, [k1, p1] 7 times, cast on 9 sts—
52 sts in rnd, 9 sts on hold for thumb.

**Next rnd** Beg with st 6, work to end of chart rnd 8, [k1, p1]
9 times, pm for new beg of rnd.

Rep rnds 1–8 of chart once more, working rib pat across palm
as established. When rnd 8 is complete, work 3 rnds in k1, p1
rib. Bind off loosely in rib.

Thumb

Place 9 thumb sts on dpn. Pick up and k 9 sts along thumb
opening—18 sts. Divide sts over 3 dpn. Work 6 rnds in k1, p1
rib. Bind off loosely in rib.

RIGHT GLOVE

Work same as for left glove to divide for thumb.

**Next rnd** Work rnd 7 of chart, [k1, p1] twice, place last 9 sts
worked on st holder for thumb.

**Next rnd** Work rnd 8 of chart over 29 sts, cast on 9 sts,
[k1, p1] 7 times—52 sts.

Complete as for left glove.

FINISHING

Fold hem to WS along picot rnd and sew in place. Weave in
ends.•

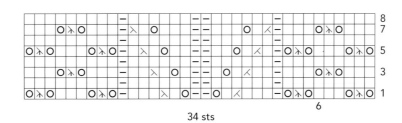

34 sts

**STITCH KEY**

☐   k on RS, p on WS     ⊙   yo     ⟋   k2tog

⊟   p on RS, k on WS     ⋏   SK2P     ⟍   SKP

# PERFORATED KNEE SOCKS

A rectangular serrated lace pattern elongates the legs of Barb Brown's irresistible knee-high socks. Knit in the round from the eyelet-detailed, ribbed cuff down, the stockinette foot is finished with a heel flap and gusset construction for long-wearing comfort in or out of shoes.

### KNITTED MEASUREMENTS
**Foot circumference** 8"/20.5cm
**Calf circumference** 10"/25.5cm
**Length (cuff to heel)** 16"/40.5cm
**Length (heel to toe)** 9"/23cm

### MATERIALS
• 2 3½oz/100g hanks (each approx 435yd/398m) of **Lorna's Laces** Shepherd Sock (superwash wool/nylon) in #56ns Fjord 🕧
• One set (4) size 1 (2.25mm) double-pointed needles (dpn), OR SIZE TO OBTAIN GAUGE
• Stitch markers

### GAUGE
36 sts and 46 rnds to 4"/10cm over St st using size 1 (2.25mm) needles.
TAKE TIME TO CHECK GAUGE.

### K2, P1 RIB
(multiple of 3 sts)
**Rnd 1** *K2, p1; rep from * around.
Rep rnd 1 for k2, p1 rib.

### SOCKS
Cast on 96 sts. Join, taking care not to twist sts, and pm for beg of rnd. Work in k2, p1 rib for 10 rnds. Knit 1 rnd, purl 1 rnd.
**Next rnd** *K2tog, yo; rep from * around.
Purl 1 rnd, knit 1 rnd.
Work in k2, p1 rib for 10 rnds.
**Next rnd** Knit, inc 2 sts evenly around—98 sts.

### Begin Charts
**Set-up rnd** K29, pm for end of shaping chart, k to end.
**Rnd 1** Work shaping chart over first 29 sts, sm, work 8-st rep of lace chart 8 times, work to end of lace chart.
Cont in this manner to work shaping chart and rep rnds 1–40 of lace chart until rnd 72 of shaping chart is complete—72 sts. Remove shaping marker.
Cont to rep rnds 71 and 72 of shaping chart and rnds 1–40 of lace chart until sock measures 14"/35.5cm from beg, end with a rnd 18 of lace chart.

### Heel Flap
**Note** Heel flap is worked back and forth on first 19 and last 16 sts of rnd. Rem 37 sts are on hold.
**Next row (RS)** K19, turn.
**Next row (WS)** P19, remove beg of rnd marker, k16, inc 1 st evenly across—36 sts.
**Row 1 (RS)** *Sl 1, k1; rep from * to end.
**Row 2 (WS)** Sl 1, k to end.
Rep rows 1 and 2 for 16 times more.

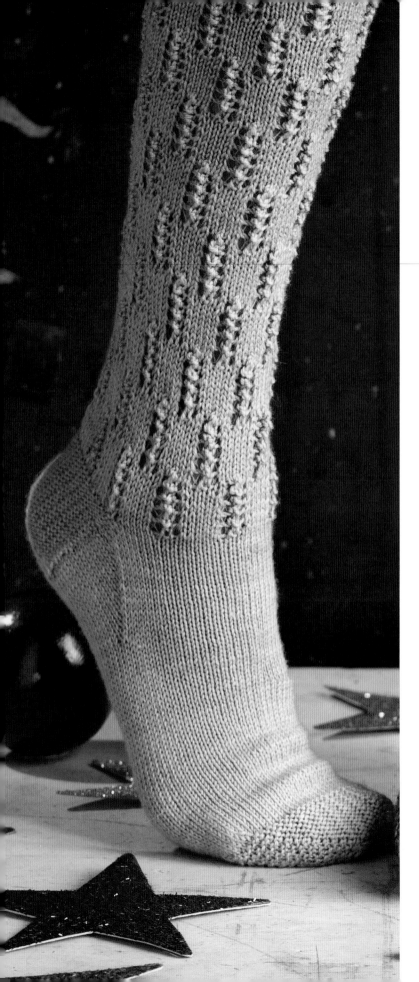

## Turn heel
**Row 1 (RS)** K18, ssk, k1, turn.
**Row 2 (WS)** Sl 1, p1, p2tog, p1, turn.
**Row 3** Sl 1, k2, ssk, k1, turn.
**Row 4** Sl 1, p3, p2tog, p1, turn.
Cont in this manner, working 1 more st before dec in each row, until 20 sts rem for heel.
**Next row (RS)** Sl 1, k17, ssk, turn.
**Next row (WS)** Sl 1, p16, p2tog, turn—18 sts.

## Gusset
**Set-up rnd** K9 heel sts, pm for new beg of rnd; with dpn #1, k9 heel sts, pick up and k 18 sts along heel flap edge; with dpn #2, k37 instep sts; with dpn #3, pick up and k 18 sts along heel flap edge, k9 heel sts—91 sts.
**Rnd 1** Knit.
**Rnd 2** With dpn #1, k to last 3 sts on needle, k2tog, k1; with dpn #2, k37 instep sts; with dpn #3, k1, ssk, k to end of rnd.
Rep last 2 rnds 8 times more—73 sts.
Work even in St st (k every rnd) until sock measures 7½"/19cm from back of heel, or 1½"/4cm less than desired length of finished foot from heel to toe.

## Toe
**Set-up rnd** With dpn #1, k to last 3 sts on needle, k2tog, k1; with dpn #2, k1, ssk, k to last 3 sts on needle, k2tog, k1; with dpn #3, k to end of rnd—70 sts.
**Rnd 1** With dpn #1, *sl 1 wyib, k1, rep from * to last 3 sts on needle, k2tog, k1; with dpn #2, k1, ssk, **sl 1 wyib, k1, rep from ** to last 3 sts on needle, k2tog, k1; with dpn #3, k1, ssk, ***k1, sl 1 wyib; rep from *** to end—4 sts dec'd.
**Rnd 2** Purl.
**Rnd 3** With dpn #1, *sl 1 wyib, k1, rep from * to last 3 sts on needle, k2tog, k1; with dpn #2, k1, k2tog, **k1, sl 1 wyib, rep from ** to last 3 sts on needle, k2tog, k1; with dpn #3, k1, k2tog, ***sl 1 wyib, k1, rep from *** to end—4 sts dec'd.
**Rnd 4** Purl.
Rep rnds 1–4 for 4 times more—30 sts.
Rep rnds 1 and 2 once more—26 sts.
With dpn #3, purl sts from dpn #1—13 sts on each of 2 dpn.
Break yarn.

## FINISHING
Graft toe using Kitchener stitch (see page 164). Weave in ends. Block to measurements.•

## LACE CHART

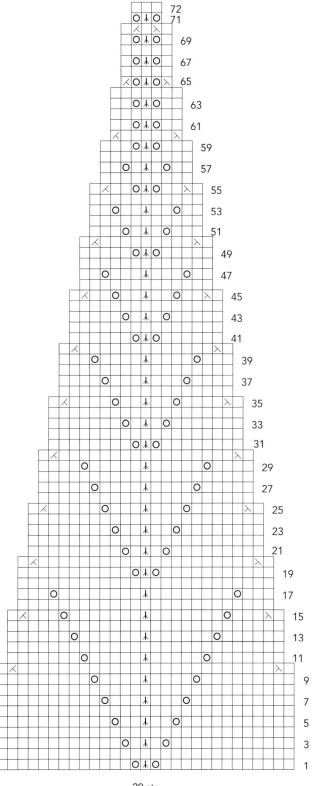

├— 8-st rep —┤

## SHAPING CHART

29 sts

## STITCH KEY

☐ k

⊟ p

◪ k2tog

◪ ssk

⊡ yo

⊼ S2KP

⊞ [yo] twice (on foll row: k1, dropping extra yo)

# LACE OVERLAY TURTLENECK

Jenifer Stark's eye-catching, close-fitting lace turtleneck is a two-layer marvel of construction. The inner layer is stockinette stitch and features a striking high turtleneck that folds over, and the outer layer features long lines of dropped-stitch lace in a lighter yarn. The two layers are joined with ribbing in finishing.

■■■▶

### SIZES
X-Small (Small/Medium, Large).
Shown in size X-Small.

### KNITTED MEASUREMENTS
**Bust** 31½ (37, 43)"/80 (94, 109)cm
**Length** 23 (23½, 24)"/58.5 (59.5, 61)cm
**Upper arm** 10½ (12, 13¾)"/26.5 (30.5, 35)cm

### MATERIALS
• Original Yarn
3 (4, 5) 3½oz/100g hanks (each approx 400yd/360m) of **Tilli Tomas** Sock (wool/nylon) in Hilton Head (A) (2)
2 (3, 3) 3oz/85g balls (each approx 345yd/315m) of **Tilli Tomas** Symphony Lace (mohair/silk/nylon/wool/beads/glitter) in Eternal Diva (B) (1)
• Substitute Yarn
3 (4, 5) 3½oz/100g hanks (each approx 436yd/400m) of **Artyarns** Merino Cloud (fine merino/cashmere) in #376 (2)
7 (8, 9) 1¾oz/50g hanks (each approx 110yd/100m) of **Artyarns** Silk Mohair Glitter (kid mohair/silk with lurex) in #308 (1)
• One each size 8 and 9 (5 and 5.5mm) circular needles, each 24"/60cm long, OR SIZE TO OBTAIN GAUGES
• Two size 9 (5.5mm) circular needles, each 16"/40cm long

• One set (5) size 9 (5.5mm) double-pointed needles (dpn)
• Stitch holders
• Stitch markers
• Scrap yarn

### GAUGES
• 22 sts and 32 rows to 4"/10cm over St st with A using smaller needles.
• 30 sts and 28 rows to 4"/10cm over k1, p1 rib with 2 strands of A held tog using larger needles.
• 20 sts and 24 rows to 4"/10cm over St st with B using smaller needles.
• One 12-st rep of lace pat is 2¾"/7cm across, one 10-row rep of chart pat is 1½"/4cm long, with B using smaller needles.
TAKE TIME TO CHECK GAUGES.

## LACE PATTERN IN RNDS

(multiple of 12 sts)

**Rnd 1** *K2, k2tog tbl, yo, k4, yo, k2tog, k2; rep from * around.

**Rnd 2** Knit.

**Rnd 3** *K3, k2tog tbl, yo, k2, yo, k2tog, k3; rep from * around.

**Rnd 4** *K2, k2tog tbl, drop yo from previous rnd, [yo] twice, k2, drop yo from previous rnd, [yo] twice, k2tog, k2; rep from * around.

**Rnd 5** *K1, k2tog tbl, drop yo's from previous rnd, [yo] 3 times, k2, drop yo's from previous rnd, [yo] 3 times, k2tog, k1; rep from * around.

**Rnd 6** *K2, [k 1 yo, drop rem 2 yo's] from previous rnd, [yo] twice, k2, [yo] twice, [k 1 yo, drop rem 2 yo] from previous rnd, k2; rep from * around.

**Rnd 7** *K3, [k 1 yo, drop rem yo] from previous rnd, yo, k2, yo, [k 1 yo, drop rem yo] from previous rnd, k3; rep from * around.

**Rnds 8–10** Knit.

Rep rnds 1–10 for lace pat in rnds.

## LACE PATTERN IN ROWS

(multiple of 12 sts)

**Row 1 (RS)** *K2, k2tog tbl, yo, k4, yo, k2tog, k2; rep from * to end.

**Row 2** Purl.

**Row 3** *K3, k2tog tbl, yo, k2, yo, k2tog, k3; rep from * to end.

**Row 4** *P2, spp (sl 1 st, p1, pass slip st over p st), drop yo from previous row, [yo] twice, p2, drop yo from previous row, [yo] twice, p2tog, p2; rep from * to end.

**Row 5** *K1, k2tog tbl, drop yo's from previous row, [yo] 3 times, k2, drop yo's from previous row, [yo] 3 times, k2tog, k1; rep from * to end.

**Row 6** *P2, [p 1 yo, drop rem 2 yo] from previous row, [yo] twice, p2, [yo] twice, [p 1 yo, drop rem 2 yo's] from previous row, p2; rep from * to end.

**Row 7** *K3, [k 1 yo, drop rem yo] from previous row, yo, k2, yo, [k 1 yo, drop rem yo] from previous row, k3; rep from * to end.

**Row 8** Purl.

**Row 9** Knit.

**Row 10** Purl.

Rep rows 1–10 for lace pat in rows.

## NOTE

Schematic measurements represent top lace layer.

## LACE PATTERN (TOP) LAYER

### Body

With smaller circular needle and scrap yarn, cast on 140 (164, 188) sts. Join, taking care not to twist sts, and pm for beg of rnd.

**Rnd 1** K70 (82, 94) front sts, pm, k70 (82, 94) back sts.

Knit 2 more rnds with scrap yarn.

Change to B, knit until ¾"/2cm from first rnd of B.

Begin lace pattern

**Next rnd** K5, work rnd 1 of lace pat over 60 (72, 84) sts, k5, sm, k5, work rnd 1 of lace pat over 60 (72, 84) sts, k5.

Work even as established in St st (k every rnd) and lace pat, AT THE SAME TIME, when piece measures 3½"/9cm from first row of B, work side shaping as foll:

*\*\***Dec rnd** K1, k2tog, work to 3 sts before marker, ssk, k1, sm, k1, k2tog, work to 3 sts before end, ssk, k1—136 (160, 184) sts.

Work 7 rnds even.

Rep from * twice more, then rep dec rnd once more—124 (148, 182) sts.

Work even until body measures approx 8"/20.5cm from beg.

**\*\*Inc rnd** K1, yo, work to 1 st before marker, yo, k1, sm, k1, yo, work to 1 st before marker, yo, k1—128 (142, 176) sts.

Work 8 rnds even.

Rep from ** twice more—136 (160, 184) sts.

Work even until body measures approx 12¾"/32.5cm from beg, AT THE SAME TIME, when 8th rep of lace panel is finished, beg to work first and last panels each side in St st, and cont to work the 3 (4, 5) center lace panels.

Divide for front and back

**Next rnd** Bind off 4 (4, 5) sts, k to 4 (4, 5) sts before next marker, bind off 4 (4, 5) sts—60 (72, 82) sts for front; remove marker, bind off 4 (4, 5) sts, k to end—64 (76, 87) sts for back. Cut yarn. Place 64 (76, 87) sts for back to st holder.

Front armhole shaping

Join yarn to front to work next row from WS in rows.

**Next row (WS)** Purl.

**Dec row** K2, k2tog, k to last 4 sts, ssk, k2—58 (70, 80) sts.

Rep last 2 rows 7 (8, 8) times more—44 (54, 64) sts.

Work even until armhole measures 4 (4½, 5)"/10 (11.5, 12.5)cm, AT THE SAME TIME, when 10 rows of lace pat have been worked 10 times, cont in St st (k on RS, p on WS) over all sts.

Front neck shaping

**Next row (RS)** K14 (19, 24) for left front, join 2nd ball of B, k next 16 sts and place on holder, k14 (19, 24) for right front. Working both sides of neck at once, purl 1 row.

**Dec row (RS)** On left side, k to last 4 (5, 5) sts, ssk (sssk, sssk), k2; on right side, k2, k2tog (k3tog, k3tog), k to end—13 (17, 22) sts each side.

Purl 1 row.

Rep last 2 rows once more—12 (15, 20) sts each side.

**Eyelet row (RS)** On left side, k3, yo, work to last 4 sts, ssk, k2; on right side, k2, k2tog, k to last 3 sts, yo, k3.

Purl 1 row.

[Dec 1 (1, 2) sts at each neck edge on next row. Purl 1 row] 4 times—8 (11, 12) sts each side.

Rep eyelet row. Purl 1 row.

[Dec 1 (2, 2) each neck edge on next row. Purl 1 row] twice—6 (7, 8) sts each side.

**Next (eyelet) row (RS)** On left side, k3, yo, work even; on right side, k to last 3 sts, yo, k3—7 (8, 9) sts each side.

Work even until armhole measures 8½ (9, 9½)"/21.5 (23, 24)cm. Bind off.

## Back armhole shaping

Slip sts from holder to needle, join B to work next row from WS.

**Next row (WS)** Bind off 4 (4, 5) sts, p to end—60 (72, 82) sts.

Work armhole shaping as for front—44 (54, 64) sts.

Work even until armhole measures 6¼ (6½, 7)"/16 (16.5, 17.5)cm, end with a WS row.

## Back neck and shoulder shaping

**Next row (RS)** K14 (19, 24) for right back, join 2nd ball of B, k next 16 sts and place on holder, k14 (19, 24) for left back. Working both sides of neck at once, purl 1 row.

**Dec row (RS)** On right side, k2, k2tog (k3tog, k3tog), k to last 4 sts, ssk, k2; on left side, k2, k2tog, k to last 4 (5, 5) sts, k2tog tbl (k3tog tbl, k3tog tbl), k2—12 (16, 21) sts each side.

**Next dec row (WS)** On left side, p2, p2tog (p2tog, p3tog), p to last 4 sts, p2tog; on right side, p2, p2tog, p to last 4 (4, 5) sts, p2tog (p2tog, p3tog), p2—10 (14, 18) sts each side.

Rep last 2 rows 1 (2, 2) times more—6 (4, 6) sts each side.

### For sizes X-Small and Large only

**Next dec row (RS)** On each side, k1, k2tog, k2tog, k1—4 sts each side.

### For all sizes

**Next dec row (WS)** One left side, P1, p3tog; on right side, p3tog, p1.

**Next dec row (RS)** On each side, k2tog and fasten off.

## Sleeves

With dpn and scrap yarn, cast on 36 (38, 40) sts. Join, taking care not to twist sts, and pm for beg of rnd. Knit 3 rnds with scrap yarn.

Change to B. Knit until ¾"/2cm from first row of B.

## Begin lace pattern

**Note** Change to larger circular needle when needed to accommodate number of sts.

**Next rnd** K6 (1, 2), work rnd 1 of pat over 24 (36, 36) sts, k6 (1, 2).

Cont in lace pat and St st as established, AT THE SAME TIME, when sleeve measures 3"/7.5cm, shape sleeves as foll:

**Inc rnd** K1, yo, k to last st, yo, k1—38 (40, 42) sts.

Rep inc rnd, working inc'd sts into St st, every 14th (10th, 8th) rnd 5 (8, 10) times more—48 (56, 62) sts. Knit 1 rnd.

Work even until sleeve measures 16 (16½, 17)"/40.5 (42, 43)cm from first row of B, AT THE SAME TIME, when 10 rows of lace pat have been worked 10 times, cont in St st only.

## Cap shaping

**Next rnd** Bind off 4 (4, 5) sts, k to end. Remove marker, beg to work in rows.

**Next row (WS)** Bind off 4 (4, 5) sts, p to end—40 (48, 52) sts.

**Next dec row** K2, k2tog, k to last 4 sts, ssk, k2—34 sts.

**Next row** Purl.

Rep last 2 rows 12 (13, 15) times more—14 (20, 20) sts.

Bind off 2 sts at beg of next 2 (4, 4) rows. Bind off rem 10 (12, 12) sts.

## STOCKINETTE (UNDER) LAYER

### Body

With smaller circular needle and scrap yarn, cast on 166 (198, 230) sts. Join, taking care not to twist sts, and pm for beg of rnd.

**Rnd 1** K83 (99, 115) front sts, pm, k83 (99, 115) back sts.

Knit 2 more rnds with scrap yarn.

Change to A, knit until 3½"/9cm from first rnd of A.

*****Dec rnd** [K1, k2tog, k to 3 sts before marker, ssk, k1, sm] twice—162 (194, 226) sts.

Work 9 rnds even.

Rep from * twice more, then work dec rnd once more—150 (182, 214) sts.

Work even until body measures approx 8"/20.5cm from beg.

******Inc rnd** K1, yo, k to 1 st before marker, yo, k1, sm, k1, yo, work to 1 st before marker, yo, k1—154 (186, 218) sts.

Work 10 rnds even.

Rep from ** twice more—162 (194, 226) sts.

Work even until body measures approx 12¾"/32.5cm from beg.

### Divide for front and back

**Next rnd** Bind off 5 (5, 6) sts, k to 5 (5, 6) sts before next marker, bind off 5 (5, 6) sts—71 (87, 101) sts for front; remove marker, bind off 5 (5, 6) sts, k to end—76 (92, 107) sts for back. Cut yarn. Sl 76 (92, 107) sts for back to st holder.

### Front armhole shaping

Join A to front to work next row from WS.

**Next row (WS)** Purl.

**Dec row** K2, k2tog, k to last 4 sts, ssk, k2—69 (85, 99) sts.

Rep last 2 rows 7 (9, 8) times more—55 (67, 83) sts.

Work even until armhole measures 4 (4½, 5)"/10 (11.5, 12.5)cm.

### Front neck shaping

**Next row (RS)** K18 (24, 32) for left front, join 2nd ball of A, k next 19 sts and place on holder, k18 (24, 32) for right front. Working both sides of neck at once, purl 1 row.

**Dec row (RS)** On left side, k to last 4 sts, ssk (ssk, sssk), k2; on right side, k2, k2tog (k2tog, k3tog), k to end—17 (23, 30) sts each side.
Purl 1 row.
Rep last 2 rows 2 (1, 3) times more—15 (22, 24) sts each side.
*Eyelet row (RS)** On left side, k3, yo, work to last 4 sts, ssk, k2; on right side, k2, k2tog, k to last 3 sts, yo, k3.
Purl 1 row.
[On next row, dec 1 (2, 2) sts at each neck edge as before. Purl 1 row] 3 times—12 (16, 18) sts each side.
Rep from * once more—9 (10, 12) sts each side.
Rep eyelet row once more.
Work even until armhole measures 8½ (9, 9½)"/21.5 (23, 24)cm.
Bind off.

Back armhole shaping
Slip sts from holder to needle, rejoin A and work next row from WS.
**Next row (WS)** Bind off 5 (5, 6) sts, p to end—71 (87, 101) sts.
Cont armhole shaping same as for front—55 (67, 83) sts.
Work even until armhole measures 6 (6½, 7)"/15 (16.5, 18)cm, end with a WS row.

Back neck and shoulder shaping
**Next row (RS)** K18 (24, 32) for right back, join 2nd ball of A, k next 19 sts and place on holder, k18 (24, 32) for left back.
Working both sides at once, purl 1 row.
**Dec row 1 (RS)** On right side, k2, k2tog (k2tog, k3tog), k to last 4 sts, ssk, k2; on left, k2, k2tog, k to last 4 (4, 5) sts, ssk (ssk, sssk), k2—16 (22, 29) sts each side.
**Dec row 2 (WS)** On left, p2, p2tog (p2tog, p3tog), p to end; on right, p to last 4 (4, 5) sts, p2tog (p2tog, p3tog), p2—15 (21, 27) sts each side.
**Dec row 3 (RS)** On right, k2, k2tog (k3tog, k3tog), k to last 4 sts, ssk, k2; on left, k2, k2tog, k to last 4 (5, 5) sts, ssk (sssk, sssk), k2—13 (18, 24) sts each side.
**Dec row 4 (WS)** On left, p2, p2tog (p3tog, p3tog), p to end; on right, p to last 4 (5, 5) sts, p2tog (p3tog, p3tog), p2—12 (16, 22) sts each side.
Rep dec rows 3 and 4 twice more—6 (6, 12) sts each side.

*For sizes X-Small and Small/Medium only*
**Next dec row (RS)** On each side, k2, k2tog, k2—5 sts each side.

*For size Large only*
**Next dec row (RS)** On each side, k1, (k3tog) 3 times, k2tog—5 sts each side.

*For all sizes*
**Next dec row (WS)** On each side, p1, p3tog, p1—3 sts each side.
**Next dec row (RS)** On each side, k3tog and fasten off.

Sleeves
With shorter circular needle and scrap yarn, cast on 42 (46, 48) sts. Join, taking care not to twist sts, pm for beg of rnd.
Knit 3 rnds with scrap yarn.
Change to A. Knit until 3"/7.5cm from first row of A.
*Inc rnd** K1, yo, k to last st, yo, k1—44 (48, 50) sts.
Rep inc rnd every 18th (14th, 8th) row 3 (7, 4) times, then every 20th (0, 10th) row 2 (0, 7) times more—54 (62, 72) sts.
Work even until sleeve measures 16 (16½, 17)"/40.5 (42, 43)cm from first row of A.

Cap shaping
**Next rnd** Bind off 5 (5, 6) sts, k to end. Remove marker, begin to work in rows.
**Next row (WS)** Bind off 5 (5, 6) sts, p to end—44 (52, 60) sts.
**Dec row** K2, ssk, k to last 4 sts, k2tog, k2—42 (50, 58) sts.
**Next row** Purl.
Rep last 2 rows 14 (17, 20) times more—14 (16, 18) sts.

*For sizes X-Small and Small/Medium only*
Rep dec row every 4th row once more—12 (14) sts.

*For size Large only*
**Next dec row** K2, sssk, k to last 5 sts, k3tog, k2—14 sts.
**Next row** Purl.

*For all sizes*
Bind off.

FINISHING
Block pieces gently to measurements.
Working each layer separately, sew bound-off shoulder edges of front to shaped shoulder edges of back. Note that front shoulder falls to back.
Pin sleeves into armholes, centering top of sleeve along front armhole edge that falls to back. Set in sleeves.
Place lace layer over St st layer, pull St st sleeves completely through lace layer. Be sure to center sleeves and body of both layers before joining with ribbing.

Hem
Working with one layer at a time, carefully remove scrap yarn and place sts on appropriate size circular needle, ready to work from original beg of rnd—166 (198, 230) sts of St st layer, 140 (164, 188) sts of lace panel layer.
With RS facing, size 9 (5.5mm) needles and one strand of A, join layers as foll:
*[K tog 1 st from each layer] 5 (4, 4) times, k 1 st from St st layer only; rep from * 25 (33, 41) times more, end [k tog 1 st from each layer] 10 (28, 20) times—166 (198, 230) sts.
Pm and join to work in rnds. With 2 strands of A held tog, work in rnds of k1, p1 rib until hem measures 2¼"/5.5cm.
Bind off loosely in rib.

## Sleeve Cuffs

Work in same manner as for hem—42 (46, 48) sts of St st layer, 36 (38, 40) sts of lace panel layer. Join layers as foll: *[K tog 1 st from each layer] 6 times, k 1 st from St st layer only; rep from * 5 (7, 7) times more, then for size Medium only, [k tog 1 st from each layer] 6 (4, 5) times—42 (46, 48) sts. Place marker and join to work in rnds. With 2 strands of A held tog, work in rnds of k1, p1 rib until cuffs measure 1¾"/4.5cm. Bind off loosely in rib.

## Collar

Work from St st layer as foll: Beg at left shoulder, with 16"/40cm circular needle and 1 strand of A, pick up and k 24 sts along left front neck edge, k 19 sts from front holder, pick up and k 24 sts along right front neck edge, 8 sts along right back neck edge, 19 sts from back holder, and 8 sts along left back neck edge—102 sts.

With 2nd 16"/40 cm circular needle, work from lace layer as foll: With 1 strand of B, pick up and k 24 sts along left front neck edge, *M1, k 8 sts from holder, M1, k 8 sts from holder, M1*, pick up and k 24 sts along right front neck edge, 8 sts along right back neck edge, rep between *s once, pick up and k 8 sts along left back neck edge—102 sts. Cut B. Pm and join to work in rnds. With RS facing, size 9 (5.5mm) needles and one strand of A, join layers by k tog 1 st from each layer all around. With 2 strands of A held tog, work in rnds of k1, p1 rib until collar measures 10"/25.5cm. Bind off loosely in rib. Weave in ends.•

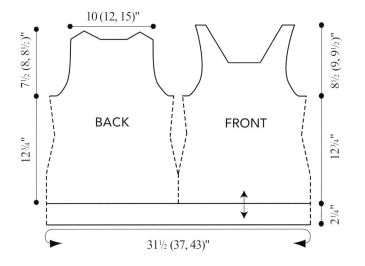

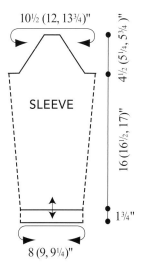

# GULL-WING LACE COWL

Lace doesn't have to be complicated to shine, as demonstrated by Faith Hale's gull-wing lace cowl. Worked in the round, a neutral shade of mohair yarn with a visible halo allows the lace to open up beautifully, giving you a go-with-everything, multi-season piece.

## KNITTED MEASUREMENTS
**Circumference** 28"/71cm
**Length** 11½"/29cm

## MATERIALS
• Original Yarn
2 1¾oz/50g balls (each approx 98yd/90m) of **Bergère de France** Mohair (mohair/polyamide/wool) in #243.22 Souffle (5)
• Substitute Yarn
2 hanks (each approx 145yd/130m) of **Halcyon Yarn** Victorian Brushed Mohair (mohair/wool/nylon) in #1060 (5)
• One size 9 (5.5mm) circular needle, 24"/60cm long, OR SIZE TO OBTAIN GAUGE
• Stitch marker

## GAUGE
14 sts and 25 rnds to 4"/10cm over lace pat using size 9 (5.5mm) needle.
TAKE TIME TO CHECK GAUGE.

## LACE PATTERN
(multiple of 7 sts)
**Rnd 1** *K1, k2tog, yo, k1, yo, ssk, k1; rep from * around.
**Rnd 2** Knit.
**Rnd 3** *K2tog, yo, k3, yo, ssk; rep from * around.
**Rnd 4** Knit.
Rep rnds 1–4 for lace pat.

## COWL
Cast on 98 sts. Join, taking care not to twist sts, and pm for beg of rnd.
Work in lace pat for 11½"/29cm, end with a row 4. Bind off loosely.

## FINISHING
Weave in ends. Block to measurements.•

# FLOWER PETALS LACE PONCHO

Intricate and inventive, Shiri Mor's gorgeous poncho-style piece is crafted from lace medallions that are knitted separately and assembled in finishing. Partial and half-squares form the "lapels" and straight back neck, respectively.

## KNITTED MEASUREMENTS
**Width** 53¾"/136.5cm
**Length** 26¾"/68cm

## MATERIALS
• 18 1¾oz/50g balls (each approx 136yd/125m) of **Patons** Grace in #62008 Natural **(3)**
• One set (5) size 4 (3.5mm) double-pointed needles (dpn), OR SIZE TO OBTAIN GAUGE
• One size G/6 (4mm) crochet hook
• Stitch markers
• Scrap yarn
• Tapestry needle

## GAUGE
1 square is 10¾"/27.5cm square, after blocking, using size 4 (3.5mm) needles.
TAKE TIME TO CHECK GAUGE.

## NOTES
**1)** Poncho is made of 24 squares that are grafted together to form a large square with an opening in the center. The back neck is one half-square grafted to the center, and the front neck is made up of 2 quarter-squares.
**2)** Full squares are worked in the round, half and quarter-squares are worked back and forth in rows.

## PONCHO
### Square (make 24)
Cast on 8 sts leaving a long tail. Knit 1 row. Divide sts evenly over 4 dpn. Join, taking care not to twist sts, and pm for beg of rnd. Purl 1 rnd.

Begin chart 1
**Rnd 1 (RS)** Reading chart from right to left, beg with first st between red rep lines, work only sts between rep lines 4 times around.
Cont to work chart in this manner until rnd 43 is complete—46 sts in each rep, 184 sts total.
Cut yarn. Place sts on scrap yarn.
With tapestry needle, weave cast-on tail through cast-on sts and pull tight.
Block square to 10¾"/27.5cm square.

### Half-Square (make 1)
Cast on 7 sts, leaving a long tail. Knit 2 rows.

Begin chart 1
**Row 1 (RS)** Reading RS row from right to left, beg with first st and work across entire row once.
**Row 2 (WS)** Reading chart from left to right, beg with first st and work across entire row once.
Cont to work chart in this manner until row 43 is complete—92 sts.
Cut yarn. Place sts on scrap yarn.
With tapestry needle, weave cast-on tail through cast-on sts and pull tight.
Block half-square to measure 10¾ x 5½"/27.5 x 14cm.

### Quarter-Square (make 2)
Cast on 5 sts, leaving a long tail. Knit 2 rows.

Begin chart 2
**Row 1 (RS)** Reading chart from right to left, beg with first st and work across entire row.
**Row 2 (WS)** Reading chart from left to right, beg with first st and work across entire row.

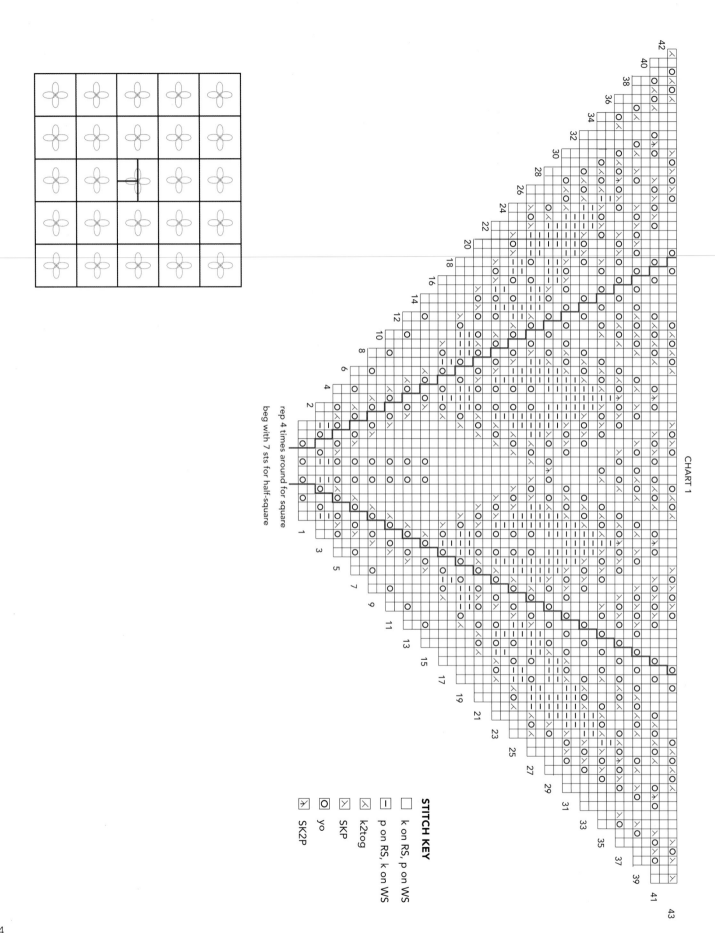

CHART 1

rep 4 times around for square
beg with 7 sts for half-square

**STITCH KEY**

☐ k on RS, p on WS

☐ p on RS, k on WS

╲ k2tog

╱ SKP

O yo

⋏ SK2P

Cont to work chart in this manner until row 43 is
complete—47 sts.
Cut yarn. Place sts on scrap yarn.
With tapestry needle, weave cast-on tail through cast-on sts
and pull tight.
Block quarter-square to measure 5½"/14cm square.

FINISHING
Foll assembly diagram, use Kitchener stitch or 3-needle bind-
off (see page 164) to graft pieces together.
Center stitch of quarter square can be joined with either side.
With crochet hook, work 1 row half double crochet (hdc) (see
page 165) around entire edge of poncho, working 1 st into
each open lp, and 3 sts in each open corner lp.
Iron entire piece flat.•

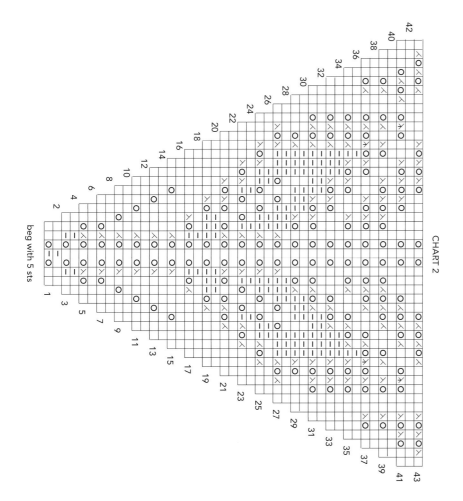

CHART 2

beg with 5 sts

# WENDING FERN SCARF

Wrapped, knotted, draped, belted: the possibilities with Lisa Hoffman's long and versatile scarf are endless. A central fern lace pattern wends its way down the center, flanked by elegant panels of right- and left-leaning leaves. The ends are capped with borders of broken ribbing.

## KNITTED MEASUREMENTS
Approx 11 x 60"/28 x 152.5cm

## MATERIALS
• Original Yarn
1 8¾oz/250g hank (approx 549yd/502m) of **Alpaca with a Twist** Baby Twist (alpaca) in #3004 Baby Pink (3)
• Substitute Yarn
5 1¾oz/50g hanks (each approx 109yd/100m) of **Debbie Bliss** Aymara (baby alpaca) in #11 Quartz (3)
• One pair size 4 (3.5mm) needles, OR SIZE TO OBTAIN GAUGES

## GAUGES
• 23 sts and 32 rows to 4"/10cm over broken rib, after blocking, using size 4 (3.5mm) needles.
• 22 sts and 28 rows to 4"/10cm over chart, after blocking, using size 4 (3.5mm) needles.
TAKE TIME TO CHECK GAUGES.

## BROKEN RIB
(multiple of 6 sts plus 3)
**Row 1 (RS)** K1, *p1, k1; rep from * to end.
**Row 2** P3, *k3, p3; rep from * to end.
Rep rows 1 and 2 for broken rib.

## SCARF
Cast on 63 sts.
Work in broken rib pat for 2"/5cm.
Rep rows 1–8 of chart pat until scarf measures approx 58"/147cm from beg, end with chart row 4.
Work in broken rib pat for 2"/5cm. Bind off loosely.

## FINISHING
Weave in ends. Block lightly to measurements.•

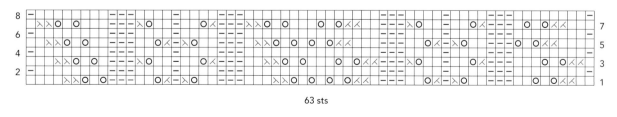

63 sts

**STITCH KEY**   □ k on RS, p on WS   — p on RS, k on WS   ⊙ yo   ◪ k2tog   ◩ ssk

# LACE JACKET

Brooke Nico's ethereal, Victorian-inspired lace jacket is a pentagon knit from the center out with a single piece forming the shawl collar and curving body. The entire jacket is bordered with a traditional scallop lace pattern. Close-fitting stockinette sleeves finish in lace cuffs.

■■■■▬

## SIZES
X-Small (Small/Medium, Large, X-Large). Shown in X-Small.

## KNITTED MEASUREMENTS
**Diameter (when flat)** 37 (37, 38½, 39)"/94 (94, 98, 99)cm
**Upper arm** 12¼ (14½, 17, 18)"/31 (37, 43, 45.5)cm

## MATERIALS
• 4 (5, 5, 5)  0.88oz/25g balls (each approx 269yd/245m) of **Filatura di Crosa/ Tahki•Stacy Charles, Inc.** Baby Kid Extra (mohair/ polyamide) in #324 Navy ①
• Four size 5 (3.75mm) circular needles, one each 16"/40cm, 24"/60cm, 40"/100cm, and 60"/150cm long, OR SIZE TO OBTAIN GAUGE
• Six size 5 (3.75mm) double-pointed needles (dpn)
• Two size 4 (3.5mm) dpn
• 5 stitch markers in different colors
• Smooth, contrasting scrap yarn in a similar weight

## GAUGE
20 sts and 32 rows to 4"/10cm over St st using size 5 (3.75mm) needle.
TAKE TIME TO CHECK GAUGE.

## NOTES
**1)** Jacket is worked in the round from the center outward. The lace edge is added to body after chart 2 has been worked.
**2)** Change from dpn to increasingly longer circular needles throughout to accommodate the growing number of stitches.

## BODY
With larger dpn and main yarn, cast on 5 sts and divide evenly over 5 dpn. Join, taking care not to twist sts, and pm for beg of rnd.
**Rnd 1** Knit.
**Rnd 2** *K1, yo; rep from * around—10 sts.
**Rnds 3 and 4** Rep rnds 1 and 2—20 sts.
**Rnd 5** Knit.

### For Sizes XS, S/M Only
**Rnd 6** [K1, yo, k3, yo, pm] 5 times—30 sts.
**Rnds 7 and 8** Knit.
**Rnd 9** [K1, yo, k to marker, yo, sm] 5 times—10 sts inc'd.
**Rnds 10 and 11** Knit.
**Rnds 12–17** Rep rnds 9–11 twice—60 sts total, 12 sts in each section.

### For Sizes L, XL Only
**Rnd 6** *K1, yo; rep from * around—40 sts.
**Rnds 7 and 8** Knit.
**Rnd 9** [K2, yo, k5, yo, k1, pm] 5 times around—50 sts.
**Rnds 10 and 11** Knit.
**Rnd 12** [K2, yo, k to 1 st before next marker, yo, k1, sm] 5 times around—10 sts inc'd.
**Rnds 13–15** Rep rnds 10–12—70 sts total, 14 sts in each section.
**Rnds 16 and 17** Knit.

### For Size XL Only
**Rnd 18** Rep rnd 12—80 sts total, 16 sts in each section.
**Rnds 19 and 20** Knit.

### Begin Chart 1
For sizes X-Small and Small/Medium only
**Rnd 1** Work sts between blue lines five times around—14 (14) sts in each section.

For size Large only
**Rnd 1** Work sts between green lines five times around—16 sts in each section.

### For size X-Large only

**Rnd 1** *Beg as indicated and work first set of sts between red lines, then work sts between red lines in center of chart, then work last set of sts between red lines, end as indicated; rep from * a total of five times around—18 sts in each section.

### For all sizes

Cont to work chart 1 as established, changing to circular needle when sts no longer fit comfortably on dpn, until rnd 37 has been worked—38 (38, 40, 42) in each section.

### Separate for Armholes

### For size X-Small only

**Rnd 1** Knit.

**Rnd 2** K to marker, sm, *k4, then with scrap yarn k30, sl these 30 sts back to LH needle and k again with main yarn*, [k to marker, sm] twice, rep from * to * once more, k to end.

**Rnd 3** [K1, yo, k to next marker, yo, sm] 5 times around.

**Rnds 4 and 5** Knit.

**Rnds 6–11** Rep rnds 3–5 twice—44 sts in each section.

### For size Small/Medium only

**Rnds 1 and 2** Knit.

**Rnd 3** [K1, yo, k to marker, yo, sm] 5 times around.

**Rnds 4 and 5** Knit.

**Rnd 6** [K1, yo, k to marker, yo, sm] 5 times around.

**Rnd 7** Knit.

**Rnd 8** K to marker, sm, *k3, then with scrap yarn k36, sl these 36 sts back to LH needle and k again with main yarn*, [k to marker, sm] twice, rep from * to * once more, k to end.

**Rnd 9** Rep rnd 6 once—44 sts in each section.

**Rnds 10 and 11** Knit.

### For size Large only

**Rnds 1 and 2** Knit.

**Rnd 3** [K2, yo, k to 1 st before marker, yo, k1, sm] 5 times around.

**Rnds 4–9** Rep rnds 1–3 twice.

**Rnd 10** Knit.

**Rnd 11** K to marker, sm, *k2, then with scrap yarn k42, sl these 42 sts back to LH needle and k again with main yarn*, [k to marker, sm] twice, rep from * to * once more, k to end.

### For size X-Large only

**Rnds 1 and 2** Knit.

**Rnd 3** [K2, yo, k to 1 st before marker, yo, k1, sm] 5 times around.

**Rnds 4–9** Rep rnds 1–3 twice.

**Rnd 10** Knit.

**Rnd 11** K to marker, sm, *k2, then with scrap yarn k44, sl these 44 sts back to LH needle and k again with main yarn*, [k to marker, sm] twice, rep from * to * once more, k to end.

### Begin Chart 2

Work same as for Chart 1, beg and end as indicated for each size on chart 2, work rnd 1 five times around—46 (46, 48, 50) sts in each section.

Cont to work chart 2 as established until rnd 52 has been worked—80 (80, 82, 84) sts in each section.

**Rnds 53 and 54** Knit—400 (400, 410, 420) sts total.

### Lace Edge

**Note** Lace edge is joined to body at the end of every WS row by working k2tog tbl over last st of lace edge tog with next st of body, so for each body st worked, 2 rows of chart 3 are worked. To work lace edge around the 5 points of shawl body, multiple rows will be worked in corner sts as indicated for each size.

**4-Row Corner** Work to end of WS row and join sts and drop the lace edge st but do not drop the body st from LH needle. Turn and work next RS and WS rows, joining sts and allowing body st to drop from needle. Turn and work next RS row—4 rows have been joined to 1 body st.

**6-Row Corner** Work to end of WS row and join sts and drop the lace edge st but do not drop the body st from LH needle. Turn and work next RS row. Turn and work to end of next WS row and join sts and drop the lace edge st but do not drop body st from LH needle. Turn and work next RS and WS rows, joining sts and allowing body st to drop from needle. Turn and work next RS row—6 rows have been joined to 1 body st.

### Begin chart 3

With RS of shawl body facing and scrap yarn, cast on 21 sts onto LH needle for lace edge. With main yarn, k these sts onto RH needle of work. Turn work for WS row.

Beg with chart row 1, reading from left to right, work as foll:

### For sizes X-Small and Small/Medium only

**Joining row (WS)** *Work chart row to last lace edge st, join sts and drop the lace st but do not drop body st, then cont working a 6-row corner in first body st. Work a 4-row corner in next body st. Work 2 rows in each body st to 1 st before next marker, work a 4-row corner in that st, sm; rep from * to end of body sts, cont chart rows in sequence, working 30-row rep, ending with row 30.

### For size Large only

**Joining row (WS)** *Work chart row to last lace edge st, join sts and drop the lace st but do not drop body st, then continue working a 6-row corner in first body st. Work a 6-row corner st in next body st. Work a 4-row corner st in next body st. Work 2 rows in each body st to 2 sts before next marker, work a 4-row corner in next st, work a 6-row corner in last st, sm; rep from * to end of body sts cont chart rows in sequence, ending with row 30.

*For size X-Large only*
**Joining row (WS)** *Work chart row to last lace edge st, join sts and do not drop body st, then cont working a 6-row corner in first body st. Work a 4-row corner in each of next 2 body sts. Work 2 rows in each body st to 2 sts before next marker, work a 4-row corner in each of next 2 sts, sm; rep from * to end of body sts continuing chart rows in sequence, end with row 30.

*For all sizes*
Carefully remove scrap yarn and place sts on spare needle. Graft ends tog.

## SLEEVES
Work right sleeve first, carefully remove scrap yarn from sleeve opening and work as foll:
Beg at A on diagram and place 30 (36, 42, 44) sts from inner

side of opening on smaller dpn, place 31 (37, 43, 45) sts from outer side of opening on second smaller dpn. Place marker on this rnd for length.

With shortest circular needle, join main yarn, pick up and k 1 st at bottom of sleeve opening, then k sts from LH needle, pick up and k 1 st at top of sleeve opening, then k sts from RH needle, pick up and k 1 more st at bottom of sleeve opening—64 (76, 88, 92) sts. Join and pm for beg of rnd. Work sleeve sts in St st for 16 rnds.

Cont in St st and dec 1 st at beg and end of rnd on next rnd, then every 8th (6th, 6th, 6th) rnd 2 (7, 13, 9) times more, then every 6th (4th, 4th, 4th) rnd 12 (13, 4, 10) times, then dec 0 (0, 1, 1) st on next rnd—34 (34, 51, 51) sts.

Work even until sleeve measures 14 (14½, 15, 15)"/ 35.5 (37, 38, 38)cm.

Work left sleeve in same manner.

CHART 1

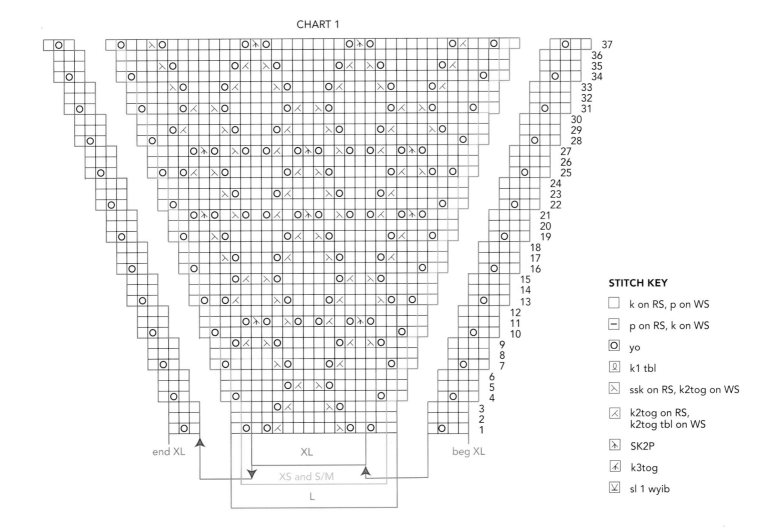

**STITCH KEY**

☐ k on RS, p on WS

─ p on RS, k on WS

O yo

Ⴍ k1 tbl

⟍ ssk on RS, k2tog on WS

⟋ k2tog on RS, k2tog tbl on WS

⋀ SK2P

⋀ k3tog

⌄ sl 1 wyib

# CHART 2 – LEFT HALF

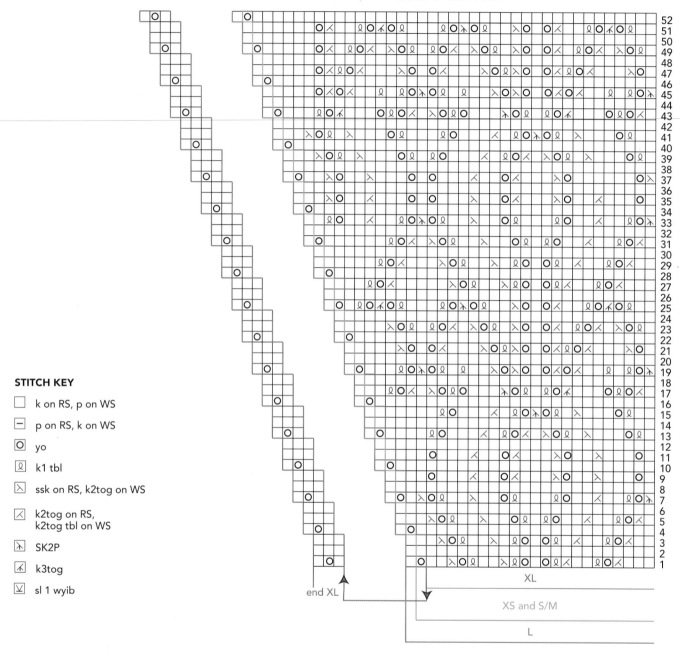

**STITCH KEY**

☐ k on RS, p on WS

⊟ p on RS, k on WS

O yo

Ω k1 tbl

⟋ ssk on RS, k2tog on WS

⟍ k2tog on RS,
   k2tog tbl on WS

⋏ SK2P

⋏ k3tog

⋎ sl 1 wyib

end XL

XL

XS and S/M

L

CHART 2 – RIGHT HALF

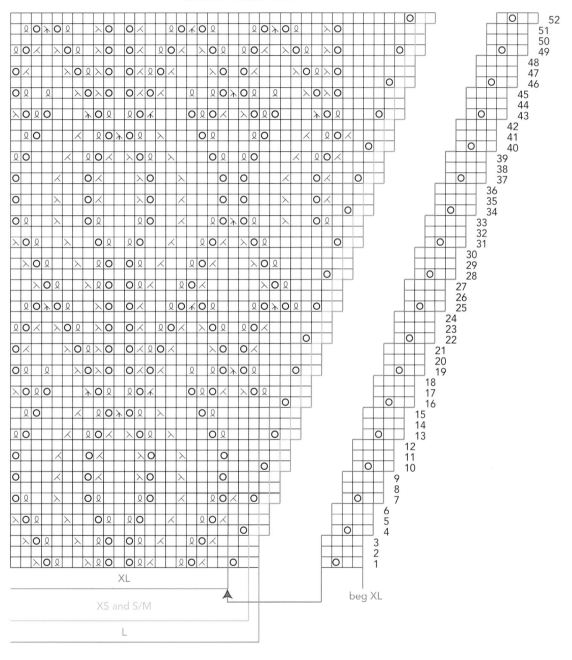

Lace Cuff

Begin chart 4

With RS of sleeve facing and scrap yarn, cast on 22 sts to LH needle for lace cuff.

Work chart 4 as for lace edge over 34-row rep, joining sts but do not work any multiple row corners, end with row 34. Carefully remove scrap yarn and place sts on spare needle. Graft ends tog.•

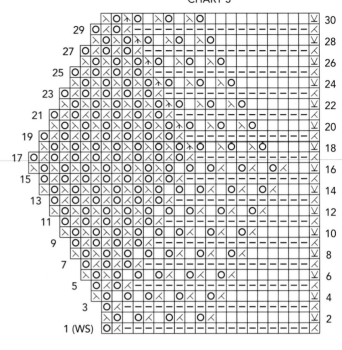

CHART 3

CHART 4

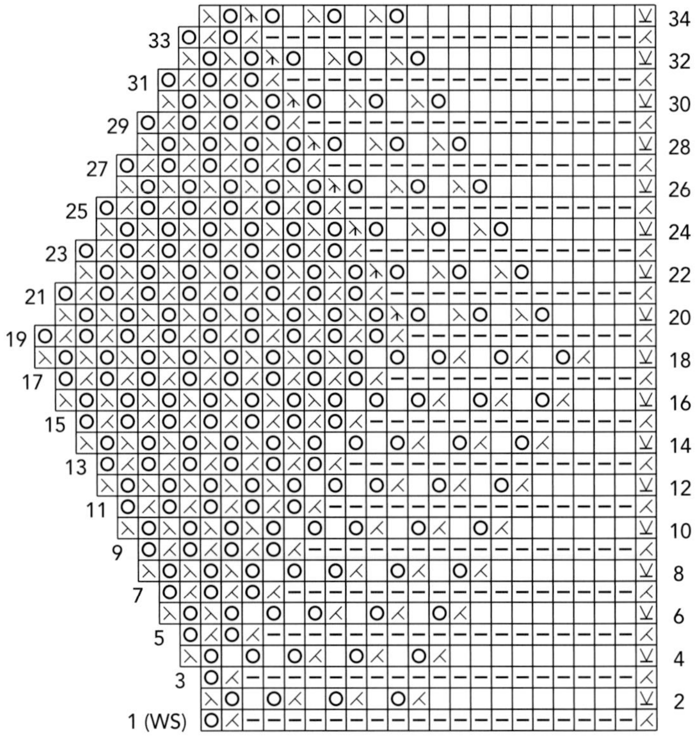

**STITCH KEY**

| | |
|---|---|
| ☐ | k on RS, p on WS |
| ⊟ | p on RS, k on WS |
| ⊙ | yo |
| ℚ | k1 tbl |
| ⊠ | ssk on RS, k2tog on WS |

| | |
|---|---|
| ⊠ | k2tog on RS, k2tog tbl on WS |
| ⋏ | SK2P |
| ⋌ | k3tog |
| ⊻ | sl 1 wyib |

# RIPPLING LACE GLOVES

Shiri Mor's stately and sumptuous opera-length fingerless gloves perfectly mesh fashion with function. A spectacular cascading lace pattern is worked throughout, and the slim shaping is achieved by switching needle sizes twice throughout the pattern.

## KNITTED MEASUREMENTS

**Arm circumference (slightly stretched)**
9"/23cm
**Hand circumference (slightly stretched)**
6"/15.5cm
**Length** 18"/45.5cm
**Note** Gloves will stretch to fit most.

## MATERIALS

• Original Yarn
1 1.4oz/40g hank (each approx 330yd/302m) of **Buffalo Gold** Lux (bison/cashmere/silk/tencel) in Huckleberry (**1**)
• Substitute Yarn
2 .88oz/25g balls (each approx 191yd/175m) of **Zealana** Air Laceweight, (down from brushtail possum fiber/cashmere/mulberry silk) in #A05 Mauve (**1**)
• One set (5) each size 0, 1, and 2 (2, 2.25, and 2.75mm) double-pointed needles (dpn), OR SIZE TO OBTAIN GAUGE
• One size 7 (4.5mm) dpn
• Stitch markers
• Stitch holder

## GAUGE

24 sts and 48 rnds to 4"/10cm, slightly stretched, using size 2 (2.75mm) needles.
TAKE TIME TO CHECK GAUGE.

**9-st rep**

**STITCH KEY**

☐ k on RS

⊟ p on RS

⊙ yo

⋏ SK2P

## GLOVE

### Palm

With size 2 (2.75mm) dpn, cast on 36 sts. Join, taking care not to twist sts, and pm for beg of rnd.
Work in k3, p3 rib for 4 rnds.

### Begin Chart

**Rnd 1** Work 9-st rep of chart 4 times.
Cont to work chart in this way until 6 rnds of chart pat are complete. Place sts on stitch holder.

### Thumb

With size 2 (2.75mm) dpn, cast on 18 sts. Join, taking care not to twist sts, and pm for beg of rnd.
Work in k3, p3 rib for 4 rnds.

### Begin Chart

**Rnd 1** Work 9-st rep of chart twice.
Cont chart in this way until 6 rnds of chart pat are complete.

### Hand and Arm

**Joining rnd** Work rnd 1 of chart pat over first 9 sts of thumb, over 36 sts from holder, over rem 9 thumb sts—54 sts.
Cont in pat until 6 rnds of chart are complete.
Change to size 1 (2.25mm) dpn.
Work rnds 1–6 of chart twice more.
Change to size 0 (2mm) dpn.
Work rnds 1–6 of chart 9 times more—12 chart reps from joining rnd.
Change to size 1 (2.25mm) dpn.
Work rnds 1–6 of chart 5 times more—17 chart reps from joining rnd.
Change to size 2 (2.75mm) dpn.
Work rnds 1–6 of chart 15 times more—32 chart reps from joining rnd.
Rep rnd 1 of chart pat.
Work 6 rnds in k3, p3 rib.
With size 7 (4.5mm) needle, bind off in rib.

### FINISHING

Weave in ends.•

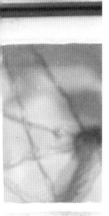
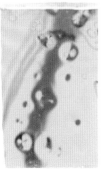

FALL 2010

# WHISPERING LACE TURTLENECK

Forget the bulk and transform a long-sleeved turtleneck with a scintillating allover lace pattern. Erica Schlueter's dreamy sheer pullover is knit flat and then sewn together. Top it off by picking up stitches for a turtleneck worked in a rib that echoes the lower hem and sleeve cuffs.

### SIZES
X-Small (Small, Medium, Large, X-Large).
Shown in size Small.

### KNITTED MEASUREMENTS
**Bust** 32 (35, 38, 40, 43)"/81 (89, 96.5, 101.5, 109)cm
**Length** 24 (24½, 25, 25½, 26)"/61 (62, 63.5, 65, 66)cm
**Upper arm** 12½ (14, 15, 15, 16½)"/32 (35.5, 38, 38, 42)cm

### MATERIALS
• Original Yarn
2 (3, 3, 3, 3) 3½oz/100g hanks (each approx 875yd/800m) of **Alpaca With a Twist** Fino (alpaca/silk) in #3001 Ruby Slippers ⬛1
• Substitute Yarn
• 4 (5, 5, 5, 6) 1¾oz/50g balls (each approx 437yd/400m) of **Willow Yarns** Stream Yarn (superwash wool/silk) in #0009 Garnet ⬛1
• One pair size 2 (2.75mm) needles, OR SIZE TO OBTAIN GAUGE
• One each sizes 1 and 2 (2.25mm and 2.75mm) circular needle, each 16"/40cm long
• One pair size 8 (5mm) needles
• Stitch markers
• Stitch holders

### GAUGE
24 sts and 44 rows to 4"/10 cm over chart, after blocking, using size 2 (2.75mm) needles.
TAKE TIME TO CHECK GAUGE.

### NOTES
**1)** When working shaping in lace pat, place markers at outer edges of lace reps to keep track of pattern. When there are not complete reps of pattern in this process, intentional elimination of a yo (with its compensating ssk or k2tog) can serve as a decrease or an additional yo can become an increase.
**2)** When working chart, work the final S2KP of the row as an ssk (over 2 sts) instead of an S2KP.
**3)** Bind off all sts very loosely.

## BACK

With size 2 (2.75mm) needles, cast on 146 (158, 170, 182, 194) sts.
Work in k1, p1 rib for 3"/7.5cm, end with a WS row.
**Dec row (RS)** K3, [k2tog, k1] 47 (51, 55, 59, 63) times, end k2—99 (107, 115, 123, 131) sts.
Purl 1 row.

### Begin Chart

**Row 1 (RS)** K1 (selvage st), work first st of chart, work 8-st rep 12 (13, 14, 15, 16) times to last st, k1 (selvage st).
**Row 2** Purl.
Cont chart in this way until rows 1–54 have been worked twice, then work rows 1–25 once more. Piece measures approx 15½"/39.5cm from beg.

### Armhole Shaping

Loosely bind off 4 sts at beg of next 2 rows—91 (99, 107, 115, 123) sts.
**Dec row (WS)** P1, p2tog, p to last 3 sts, p2tog tbl, p1.
Keeping to pat, rep dec row every WS row 3 times more—83 (91, 99, 107, 115) sts.
The next chart row is row 35. Cont in pat until armhole measures 7½ (8, 8½, 9, 9½)"/19 (20.5, 21.5, 23, 24)cm, end with a WS row. Mark center 27 (29, 31, 33, 33) sts.

### Neck and Shoulder Shaping

**Note** Work each shoulder separately while decreasing in pat by eliminating a yo or work ssk or k2tog as necessary to maintain the pat.
**Next row (RS)** Bind off 6 (7, 6, 7, 7) sts, work until there are 22 (24, 28, 30, 34) sts on RH needle, sl center 27 (29, 31, 33, 33) sts to holder, join a 2nd ball of yarn and work to end.
**Next row (WS)** Bind off 6 (7, 6, 7, 7) sts, working on the left shoulder only, and keeping to pat, cont to dec 1 st at neck edge on the next 4 RS rows, AT THE SAME TIME, shape shoulder by binding off 5 (6, 7, 7, 8) sts from shoulder edge twice, then 4 (4, 5, 6, 7) sts twice. Work the right shoulder the same way.

## FRONT

Work as for back until armhole measures 5½ (6, 6½, 7, 7½)"/14 (15, 16.5, 18, 19)cm, end with a WS row. Mark center 11 (13, 15, 17, 17) sts.

### Neck Shaping

**Next row (RS)** Work 36 (39, 42, 45, 49) sts, sl center 11 (13, 15, 17, 17) sts to a holder, join a 2nd ball of yarn and work to end.
Working each side separately, cont to shape neck, binding off

3 sts from each neck edge once, 2 sts once, then dec 1 st every WS row 7 times—24 (27, 30, 33, 37) sts rem.
Work even until armhole measures same as back.

### Shape Shoulder

Bind off 6 (7, 6, 7, 7) sts for shoulder edge once, 5 (6, 7, 7, 8) sts twice, and 4 (4, 5, 6, 7) sts twice.

## SLEEVES (make 2)

With size 2 (2.75mm) needles, cast on 64 (72, 80, 80, 88) sts.
Work in k1, p1 rib for 3"/7.5cm, end with a WS row.
**Dec row (RS)** K1 (5, 3, 3, 1), k2tog, [k3 (3, 4, 4, 5), k2tog] 12 times, k1 (5, 3, 3, 1)—51 (59, 67, 67, 75) sts.
Purl 1 row.

### Begin Chart

**Row 1 (RS)** K1 (selvage st), work first st of chart, work 8-st rep 6 (7, 8, 8, 9) times to last st, k1 (selvage st).
**Row 2** Purl.
Cont to work chart in this way, AT THE SAME TIME, inc 1 st each side (by M1 inside of selvage sts on RS rows, M1 p-st inside of selvage sts on the WS rows) every 13th row 12 times—75 (83, 91, 91, 99) sts.
Work even until piece measures approx 18"/45.5cm from beg, end with row 50 of 3rd 54-row rep.

### Cap Shaping

Bind off 4 sts at beg of the next 2 rows.
**Dec row (WS)** P1, p2tog, p to last 3 sts, p2tog tbl, p1.
Dec 1 st each side every 2nd row 3 (5, 7, 11, 13) times, dec 1 st each side every 3rd row 9 times, every 2nd row 7 times, and then every row 3 (5, 7, 3, 5) times—21 sts.
Bind off loosely using size 8 (5mm) needle.

## FINISHING

Block pieces to measurements. Sew shoulder seams. Set in sleeves. Sew side and sleeve seams. Weave in ends.

### Turtleneck

With smaller circular needle, pick up and k 96 (100, 104, 108, 108) sts evenly around. Join and pm for beg of rnd. Change to larger circular needle.
**Rnd 1** Work k1, p1 rib, inc 24 sts evenly spaced around—120 (124, 128, 132, 132) sts. Work in rnds of k1, p1 rib for 8"/20.5cm.
Bind off loosely, using size 8 (5mm) needle.•

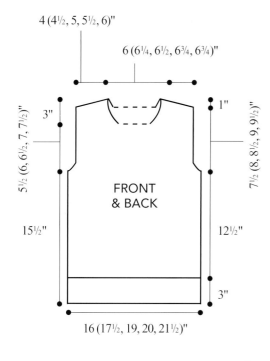

4 (4½, 5, 5½, 6)"

6 (6¼, 6½, 6¾, 6¾)"

3"

5½ (6, 6½, 7, 7½)"

1"

7½ (8, 8½, 9, 9½)"

FRONT
& BACK

15½"

12½"

3"

16 (17½, 19, 20, 21½)"

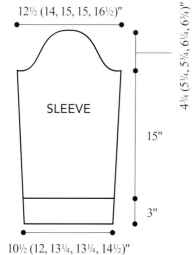

12½ (14, 15, 15, 16½)"

4¾ (5¼, 5¾, 6¼, 6¾)"

SLEEVE

15"

3"

10½ (12, 13¼, 13¼, 14½)"

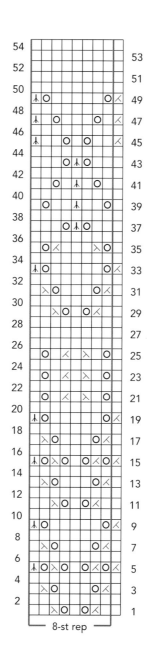

8-st rep

## STITCH KEY

☐ k on RS, p on WS

O yo

⤢ k2tog

⤡ ssk

⚹ S2KP

**Note** On reps that end in S2KP, work last rep of row (over 2 sts) as ssk

# LACE STOLE

As intricately interesting as a coral reef, Lois Young's wide lace stole is knit in a breezy, overall cable and lattice pattern edged on all sides with garter stitch borders. Knit this generous rectangular wrap in crisp, fine cotton for a springtime day at the beach.

■■■■

## KNITTED MEASUREMENTS
Approx 20 x 62½"/51 x 158.5cm

## MATERIALS
• 9  1¾oz/50g skeins (each approx 136yd/125m) **Patons** Grace (cotton) in #62009 Buff (3)
• One pair size 5 (3.75mm) needles, OR SIZE TO OBTAIN GAUGE
• Cable needle (cn)

## GAUGE
24 sts and 31 rows to 4"/10cm over chart using size 5 (3.75mm) needles.
TAKE TIME TO CHECK GAUGE.

## STITCH GLOSSARY
**2-st RPC** Sl 1 st to cn and hold to back, k1 tbl, p1 from cn.
**2-st LPC** Sl 1 st to cn and hold to front, p1, k1 tbl from cn.
**2-st RST** K1, M1, sl 2 sts just worked to LH needle and pass next st on LH needle over these sts, sl 2 sts back to RH needle.
**3-st RT** K1, yo, k1, sl 3 sts just worked to LH needle, and pass next st on LH needle over these sts, sl 3 sts back to RH needle.
**3-st CC** Sl 2 sts to cn and hold to front, k1 tbl, sl sts from cn to LH needle, sl next st back to cn and hold to front, p1, k1 tbl from cn.

## STOLE
Cast on 123 sts loosely.
Work 9 rows in garter st as foll: Sl 1 wyif, k to last st, k1 tbl.

Begin Chart
Work row 1 of chart, working 16-st rep 6 times across, work to end of chart row.
Cont to work chart pat until 44 rows have been worked 9 times, then rep rows 1–43 once more.
Work 9 rows in garter st same as for beg.
Bind off loosely.

## FINISHING
Weave in ends. Block to measurements.●

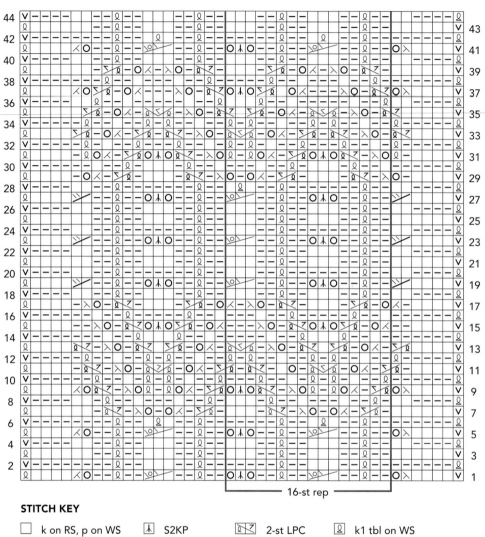

16-st rep

**STITCH KEY**

| | | | |
|---|---|---|---|
| ☐ | k on RS, p on WS | 人 S2KP | 2-st LPC | k1 tbl on WS |
| — | p on RS, k on WS | k2tog | 2-st RST | k1 tbl on RS, p1 tbl on WS |
| V | sl 1 wyif | ssk | 3-st RT | |
| O | yo | 2-st RPC | 3-st CC | |

# EVERMORE LACE TUNIC

Get ready to stand out in Brooke Nico's unique, slim-fitting cover-up. The main lace front and back sections are knit in the round from the center motif, reminiscent of a starfish, outward. The yoke is stitched top down on either side, acting as an anchor for the raglan sleeves.

## SIZES
X-Small (Small, Medium). Shown in size X-Small.

## KNITTED MEASUREMENTS
**Bust** 31 (34, 36½)"/78.5 (86, 92.5)cm
**Length (shoulder to tip of lace insert)** 34 (34½, 35)"/86 (87.5, 89)cm
**Upper arm** 12 (12¾, 13½)"/30.5 (32.5, 34.5)cm

## MATERIALS
• 6 (7, 8) 3½oz/100g skeins (each approx 220yd/201m) of **Lorna's Laces** Pearl (silk/bamboo) in Undyed (4)
• One set (5) size 6 (4mm) double-pointed needles (dpn), OR SIZE TO OBTAIN GAUGE
• Three size 6 (4mm) circular needles, each 16, 24, and 47" (40, 60 and 120cm) long
• One size I-9 (5.5mm) crochet hook
• Coil-less safety pins
• Stitch markers
• Scrap yarn

## GAUGE
22 sts and 25 rows to 4"/10cm over St st, blocked, using size 6 (4mm) needles.
TAKE TIME TO CHECK GAUGE.

## NOTES
**1)** Lace insets are knit from the center out foll charts 1, 2, and then 3. Work each rep 4 times around. Only the even-numbered rounds are shown. Work all odd-numbered rounds (except for rnd 21) as knit all sts.
**2)** After lace insets are completed, the sleeves and front and back side sections are knit from the top down with raglan shaping.
**3)** Two double decreases are used at times throughout the pattern, S2KP and SK2P. Be careful not to mix them up.

## TUNIC
Lace Inset (make 2)
Cast on 8 sts and divide evenly over 4 dpn. Join, taking care not to twist sts.

Begin chart 1
**Note** Change to 16"/40cm circular needle and place markers at each rep when sts no longer fit comfortably on dpn. Change to longer circular needles as needed.
**Rnd 1 and all odd rnds** Knit.
Cont to work chart 1 through rnd 20.
**Rnd 21** *Drop one of the yo's from previous rnd, leaving a big loop, into this loop work [k1, p1] 3 times to make 6 sts, k27; rep from * around. Cont to work chart 1, knitting all odd rnds, through round 27.

Begin chart 2
Work chart 2, knitting all odd rnds, through rnd 49.

Begin chart 3
Work chart 3 through rnd 66—320 sts.
**Rnd 67** Knit around, removing old and placing new markers as foll: k115, pm, k161, pm, k44.

Begin inset leaf edge chart
**Note** Chart is worked in rows. Odd-numbered rows are not shown on chart. Purl these rows.
**Set-up rnd** Bind off loosely 115 sts up to first marker (placing coil-less safety pin on 35th stitch bound off to mark center neck), work inset leaf edge chart over center 161 sts, bind off last 44 sts. Cut yarn.
With WS facing, join yarn to live sts.
**Row 1 and all WS rows** Purl.
Work rows 2–12 of inset leaf edge chart. Bind off loosely.

Right Raglan Yoke
Cast on 27 (31, 35) sts.
**Row 1 (WS)** P15 (17, 19) for side back, pm, p8 for sleeve, pm, p4 (6, 8) for side front.
**Row 2** K1 (3, 5), ssk, yo, k1, sm, yo, k to 1 st before marker, yo, k1, sm, yo, k2tog, k to end—29 (33, 37) sts.
**Row 3 and all WS rows** Purl.
**Row 4** K1, M1, k to 3 sts before marker, ssk yo, k1, sm, yo, k to 1 st before marker, yo, k1, sm, yo, k2tog, k to end—32 (36, 40) sts.
**Rows 6 and 8** K1, M1, k to 3 sts before marker, ssk yo, k1, sm, yo, k to 1 st before marker, yo, k1, sm, yo, k2tog, k to end.
**Row 10** K1, M1, k to 3 sts before marker, ssk, yo, k1, sm, yo, k to 1 st before marker, yo, k1, sm, yo, k2tog, k to last 3 sts, k2tog, k1. Place coil-less safety pin to mark this row for center back seam.
**Row 12** Cast on 5 sts, k10 (12, 14), ssk, yo, k1, sm, yo, k to 1 st before marker, yo, k1, sm, yo, k2tog, k9 (11, 13), k2tog, k1.
**Row 13** Purl.
**Row 14** K10 (12, 14), ssk, yo, k1, sm, yo, k to 1 st before marker, yo, k1, sm, yo, k2tog, k11 (13, 15).
Rep rows 13 and 14 for 18 (20, 22) times more—84 (92, 100) sts total with 13 (15, 17) front sts, 58 (62, 66) sleeve sts, 13 (15, 17) back sts.
Remove all markers. Work even in St st over all sts until piece measures 9 (9½, 10)"/23 (24, 25.5)cm from cast-on, end with a WS row.

Divide for sleeve and work side gussets
**Next row (RS)** K13 (15, 17), place next 58 (62, 66) sts on holder for sleeves, cast on 8 sts for underarm, k13 (15, 17).
**Row 1** P34 (38, 42).
**Row 2 (RS)** K1, ssk, k to last 3 sts, k2tog, k1.
**Rows 3, 5, 7, and 9** Purl.
**Rows 4, 6, and 8** Knit.
Rep rows 2–9 four times more, rep rows 2–7 nine times more, and then rep rows 2 and 3 for 1 (3, 5) times more—4 sts.
**Next row (RS)** K1, k2tog, k1.
**Next row** P3tog. Fasten off.

Left Raglan Yoke
Cast on 27 (31, 35) sts.
**Row 1 (WS)** P4 (6, 8) for front, pm, p8 for sleeve, pm, p15 (17, 19) for back.
**Row 2** K12 (14, 16), ssk, yo, k1, sm, yo, k to 1 st before marker, yo, k1, sm, yo, k2tog, k1.
**Row 3 and all WS rows** Purl.

**STITCH KEY**

☐  k
⊟  p
◩  k2tog
⬔  ssk
⊡  yo
⊞  [yo] twice
⬔  SK2P
⟁  S2KP
▨  no stitch
-1  remove marker, slip next st purlwise to RH needle, replace marker
-2  remove, slip next 2 sts purlwise to RH needle, replace marker

CHART 1

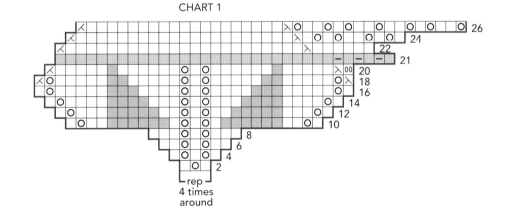

rep
4 times
around

**NOTE** On rnd 21, drop one of the loops of the double yo from rnd 20, leaving 1 big loop. Into that loop work (k1, p1) 3 times. Knit around to marker and repeat. All other odd number rounds are knit.

**Row 4** K12 (14, 16), ssk, yo, k1, sm, yo, k to 1 st before marker, yo, k1, sm, yo, k2tog, M1, k1.

**Rows 6 and 8** K12 (14, 16), ssk, yo, k1, sm, yo, k to 1 st before marker, yo, k1, sm, yo, k2tog, k to last st, M1, k1.

**Row 10** K1, ssk, k9 (11, 13), ssk, yo, k1, sm, yo, k to 1 st before marker, yo, k1, sm, yo, k2tog, k to last st, M1, k1.

**Row 12** K1, ssk, k8 (10, 12), ssk, yo, k1, sm, yo, k to 1 st before marker, yo, k1, sm, yo, k2tog, k to end, cast on 5 sts at end of row.

Complete as for right front, reversing shaping as established.

Sleeves (make 2)

With 16"/40cm circular needle, cast on 4 sts for underarm, k across 58 (62, 66) held sleeve sts, cast on 4 sts for underarm—66 (70, 74) sts. Join and pm for beg of rnd.

**Rnds 1–5** Knit.

**Dec rnd 6** Ssk, k to last 2 sts, k2tog.

Rep rnds 1–6 for 8 (6, 3) times more, then rep dec rnd 6 every 4th rnd 0 (4, 9) times—48 sts.

Work even until sleeve measures 9 (9½, 10)"/23 (24, 25.5)cm from underarm cast-on.

Begin sleeve leaf edge chart

**Note** On rnds 7, 9, and 11, remove marker, slip next st purlwise to LH needle, replace marker.

Working 8-st rep 6 times around, work rnds 1–12 twice.

Bind off all sts loosely.

FINISHING

Block pieces to measurements.

Seam center back neck yokes for approx 1"/2.5cm to marked st.

Set in back lace inset; match center back neck to marked bound-off st on lace inset and seam down to leaf lace edge of lace inset, rep for other side.

Set in front lace inset as foll: Join cast-on edge at neckline of front yoke to marked bound off st on 2nd lace inset and seam down to hem. Cont seam to join leaf lace edges of lace inset pieces.

Repeat for other side.

With size I-9 (5.5mm) crochet hook, work 1 row sl st (see page 165) in each st around neck edge.•

SLEEVE LEAF EDGE

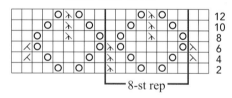

8-st rep

INSET LEAF EDGE

8-st rep

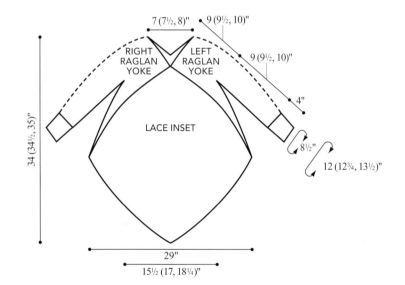

**STITCH KEY**

| | |
|---|---|
| ☐ k | ⅄ SK2P |
| ⊟ p | ⅄ S2KP |
| ⊠ k2tog | ▨ no stitch |
| ⊠ ssk | **-1** remove marker, slip next st purlwise to RH needle, replace marker |
| ☐ yo | |
| 00 [yo] twice | **-2** remove, slip next 2 sts purlwise to RH needle, replace marker |

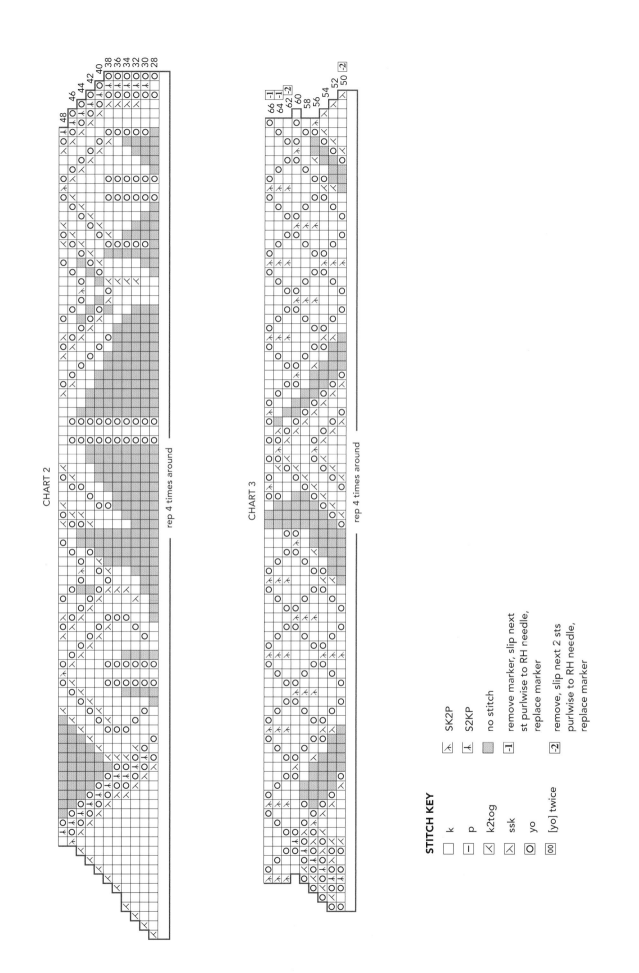

CHART 2

rep 4 times around

CHART 3

rep 4 times around

**STITCH KEY**

☐ k

— p

☒ k2tog

☒ ssk

○ yo

00 [yo] twice

⅄ SK2P

人 S2KP

▨ no stitch

-1 remove marker, slip next st purlwise to RH needle, replace marker

-2 remove, slip next 2 sts purlwise to RH needle, replace marker

# LACE BERET

There's nothing old hat about Kate Gagnon Osborn's sweet and sassy beret. You'll use two sizes of circular needles and one size of double-points to craft this French-inspired tam, worked in leafy lace from the ribbed brim to the crown.

### KNITTED MEASUREMENTS
**Brim circumference (unstretched)** Approx 17"/43cm
**Diameter** 10"/25.5cm

### MATERIALS
• Original Yarn
2  1¾oz/50 hanks (each approx 165yd/151m) of **Tilli Tomas** Milan (cashmere/silk/merino) in #20S Whisper (3)
• Substitute Yarn
1  4oz/113g hank (approx 370yd/333m) of **Squoosh Fiberarts** Merino Cashmere Sock (superwash merino/cashmere/nylon) in Special Skeins 356 (3)
• One size 2 (2.75mm) circular needle, 20"/50cm long, OR SIZE TO OBTAIN GAUGES
• One set (5) size 2 (2.75mm) double-pointed needles (dpn)
• One size 0 (2mm) circular needle, 16"/40cm long
• Stitch marker

### GAUGES
• 28 sts and 35 rnds to 4"/10cm over St st, after blocking, using larger needles.
• 30 sts and 38 rnds to 4"/10cm over chart, after blocking, using larger needles.
TAKE TIME TO CHECK GAUGES.

### BERET
With smaller circular needle, cast on 140 sts. Join, taking care not to twist sts, and pm for beg of rnd.
**Rnd 1** *[K1, p1] twice, k1, p2; rep from * around.
Rep rnd 1 until piece measures 1"/2.5cm.
**Inc rnd** *[K1, yo, p1, yo] twice, k1, p2; rep from * around—220 sts.
**Next rnd** *[K1, k1 tbl, p1, p1 tbl] twice, k1, p2; rep from * around.

### Begin Chart
Change to larger circular needle. Work 11-st rep of chart 20 times around.
Work chart through rnd 60, changing to dpn when sts no longer fit comfortably on circular needle—40 sts.
**Dec rnd** *SKP; rep from * to end—20 sts.
Rep dec rnd once more—10 sts.
Cut yarn, leaving 8"/20.5cm tail. Thread tail through rem sts and secure to close top.

### FINISHING
Weave in ends. Wet-block then stretch over a 10"/25.5cm plate to dry.•

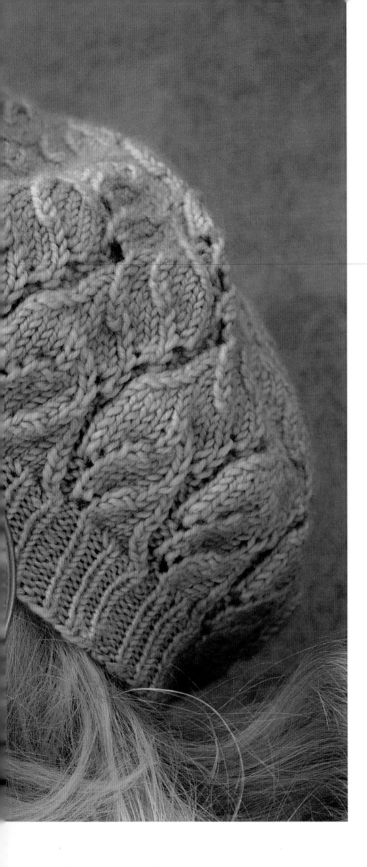

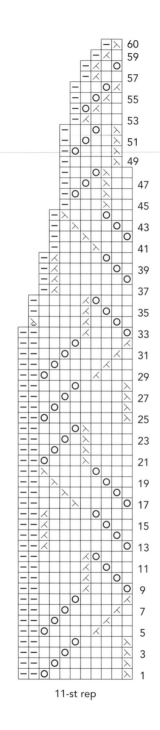

## STITCH KEY

| | |
|---|---|
| □ | k |
| − | p |
| ⊙ | yo |
| ⟋ | k2tog |
| ⟍ | skp |
| ⟑ | p2tog |

11-st rep

# WONDERSOME LACE SOCKS

Debbie O'Neill's dainty socks wouldn't be out of place in *Alice in Wonderland* with their charming details that hearken to another time. Rising to just above the ankle, they are knit from the cuff down in two different lace motifs separated by columns of eyelets that carry down into the heel flap and along the instep.

⬛⬛⬛▶

## SIZES
Woman's Small (Medium, Large).
Shown in size Medium.

## KNITTED MEASUREMENTS
**Leg circumference** Approx 6½ (7½, 8½)"/
16.5 (19, 21.5)cm

## MATERIALS
• Original Yarn
3  1¾oz/50g hanks (each approx
160yd/146m) of **Artyarns** Cashmere Sock
(cashmere/wool/nylon) in #20S Pale
Blue ②
• Substitute Yarn
3  1¾oz/50g hanks (each approx
185yd/169m) of **Kelbourne Woolens**
Andorra (merino wool/highland wool/
mohair) in #446 Haint Blue ②
• One set (4) size 1 (2.5mm) double-pointed
needles (dpn), OR SIZE TO OBTAIN GAUGE
• Stitch marker

## GAUGE
36 sts and 50 rnds to 4"/10cm over St st
using size 1 (2.5mm) needles.
TAKE TIME TO CHECK GAUGE.

## LACE INSERT
(over 4 (6, 8) sts)
**Rnd 1** P1 (2, 3), k2tog, yo, p1 (2, 3).
**Rnd 2** P1 (2, 3), k2, p1 (2, 3).
**Rnd 3** P1 (2, 3), yo, ssk, p1 (2, 3).
**Rnd 4** P1 (2, 3), k2, p1 (2, 3).
Rep rnds 1–4 for lace insert.

## SOCK
Cuff
With size 1 (2.5mm) dpn, cast on 60 (68, 76) sts and divide
evenly over 3 needles. Join, taking care not to twist sts, and
pm for beg of rnd.
**Rnd 1** [P1 (2, 3), k2, p1 (2, 3), k2, p2, k4, p1, k4, p1 (2, 3),
k2, p1 (2, 3), k4, p1, k4] twice.
**Rnd 2** [P1, k2tog, yo, p1 (2, 3), k2tog, yo, p2, k4, p1, k4, p1
(2, 3), k2tog, yo, p1 (2, 3), k4, p1, k4, p0 (1, 2)] twice.
**Rnd 3** Rep rnd 1.

ROSE CALLAHAN

**Rnd 4** [P1, yo, ssk, p1 (2, 3), yo, ssk, p2, k4, p1, k4, p1 (2, 3), yo, ssk, p1 (2, 3), k4, p1, k4, p0 (1, 2)] twice.
Rep rnds 1–4 until piece measures 2"/5cm.
Rep rnd 1 once more.

## Leg

**Next rnd** [Work rnd 1 of lace insert, work rnd 1 of chart 1, work rnd 1 of lace insert, work rnd 1 of chart 2] twice.
Cont to work in established pat foll charts and working rnds 1–4 of lace insert until sock measures approximately 8"/20.5cm or desired length from beg.

## Heel Flap

**Note** Heel flap is worked by cont chart 1 and lace insert on either side, framed by 2 sts in St st on each side. Work WS rows 2 and 4 of lace insert as foll: K1 (2, 3), p2, k1 (2, 3).
**Next.row** Work 21 (25, 29) sts in pat, k4, turn, sl 1, p3, work 21 (25, 29) sts in pat, p4. Keep rem 31 (35, 39) on hold for instep.
Cont to work back and forth on heel sts as foll:
**Next row (RS)** Sl 1, k3, work 21 (25, 29) sts in pat, k4.
**Next row** Sl 1, p3, work 21 (25, 29) sts in pat, p4.
Rep last 2 rows 12 (14, 16) times, end with WS row.
**Next row (RS)** Sl 1, k to end of row.
**Next row** Sl 1, p to end of row.
Rep rows 1 and 2 three times more, end with WS row.

## Turn heel

**Row 1** K17 (19, 21), SKP, k1, turn.
**Row 2** Sl 1, p6 (6, 7), p2tog, p1, turn.
**Row 3** Sl 1, k to 1 st before gap, SKP, k1, turn.
**Row 4** Sl 1, p to 1 st before gap, p2tog, p1, turn.
Rep rows 3 and 4 until 20 (21, 23) sts rem.

*For size Small only*
**Next row** Sl 1, k to 1 st before gap, SKP, k1, turn.
**Next row** Sl 1, p to last 2 sts, p2tog—18 sts.

*For sizes Medium and Large only*
**Next row (RS)** Sl 1, k to last 2 sts, SKP—(20, 22) sts.
Purl 1 row.

## Gusset

**Next rnd** With free needle, k9 (10, 11) heel sts, pm for new beg of rnd. With new dpn (dpn #1), k9, (10, 11) heel sts, pick up and k 16 (18, 20) sts along heel flap; with free dpn (dpn #2), work 31 (35, 39) instep sts in pat as established; with rem dpn (dpn #3), pick up and k 16 (18, 20) sts along other side of heel flap, k rem 9 (10, 11) heel sts—81 (91, 101) sts.
**Rnd 1** With dpn #1, k to last 3 sts, k2tog, k1; with dpn #2, work in pat; with dpn #3, k1, ssk, k to end.
**Rnd 2** Work even, cont pat on instep, with rem sts in St st (k every rnd).
Rep rnds 1 and 2 until 60 (68, 76) sts rem.

## Foot

Work even in pat until sock measures about 1¾ (2, 2½)"/4.5 (5, 5.5)cm shorter than desired length from heel to toe, end after an even-numbered rnd.

## Toe Shaping

**Note** Toe is worked in St st.
**Set-up rnd** With dpn #1, knit; with dpn #2, k1, ssk, k to last 3 sts, k2tog, k1; with dpn #3, knit—58 (66, 74) sts.
Knit 1 rnd.
**Rnd 1** With dpn #1, k to last 3 sts, k2tog, k1; with dpn #2, k1, ssk, k to the last 3 sts, k2tog, k1; with dpn #3, k1, ssk, k to end of rnd.
**Rnd 2** Knit.
Rep rnds 1 and 2 until 22 sts rem.

## FINISHING

Knit bottom of foot sts to one needle. Using Kitchener stitch (see page 164), graft foot sts to instep sts.•

CHART 1

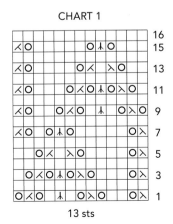

13 sts

CHART 2

9 sts

**STITCH KEY**

☐ k

⊟ p

☐O yo

◿ k2tog

◺ ssk

⊼ S2KP

# MOONFLOWER LACE DRESS

Unleash your inner flower child with Shirley Paden's flirty baby doll dress. Featuring bell sleeves, a square neckline, and a flouncing ruffled hem, the dress's narrow lace bands are knit horizontally, with larger sections either picked up from or sewn to these bands.

∎∎∎▶

### SIZES
Small (Medium, Large). Shown in size Small.

### MEASUREMENTS
**Bust** 34 (37, 40)"/86 (94, 102)cm
**Length** 32 (32½, 33)"/81 (82.5, 84)cm
**Upper arm** 12 (13, 14)"/30.5 (33, 35.5)cm

### MATERIALS
• 13 (14, 15) 1¾oz/50g balls (each approx 153yd/140m) of **Anny Blatt** Louxor (cotton) in #50 Blanc (**2**)
• One pair size 6 (4mm) needles, OR SIZE TO OBTAIN GAUGE
• Either one 40"/100cm or two 32"/80cm size 6 (4mm) circulars for Panel #1 (**Note** Use two 32"/80cm circulars for same feeling as working with 2 needles. The length is needed to accommodate the large stitch count.)

### GAUGE
20 sts and 28 rows to 4"/10cm over lacy knots pat using size 6 (4mm) needles. TAKE TIME TO CHECK GAUGE.

### Lacy Knots Pattern
(multiple of 16 sts plus 2)
**Row 1 (RS)** K1 (selvage st), *k2, yo, SK2P, yo, k11; rep from * to last st, k1 (selvage st).
**Row 2** K1, p to last st, k1.
**Row 3** K1, *k2tog, yo, p3, yo, ssk, k9; rep from * to last st, k1.
**Row 4** K1, *p10, k5, p1; rep from * to last st, k1.
**Row 5** K1, *k2, yo, SK2P, yo, k11; rep from * to last st, k1.
**Rows 6, 8, and 10** Rep row 2.
**Row 7** Knit.
**Row 9** K1, *k10, yo, SK2P, yo, k3; rep from * to last st, k1.
**Row 11** K1, *k8, k2tog, yo, p3, yo, ssk, k1; rep from * to last st, k1.
**Row 12** K1, *p2, k5, p9; rep from * to last st, k1.
**Row 13** K1, *k10, yo, SK2P, yo, k3; rep from * to last st, k1.
**Row 14** Rep row 2.
**Row 15** Knit.
**Row 16** Rep row 2.
Rep rows 1–16 for lacy knots pat.

### Acorn Edging
Cast on 8 sts.
**Row 1** Yo, p2tog, (k1, p1, k1, p1, k1) in next st, yo, p2tog, k1, [yo] 3 times, k2—15 sts.
**Row 2** K3, p1, k2, yo, p2tog, k5, yo, p2tog—15 sts.
**Row 3** Yo, p2tog, k5, yo, p2tog, k6—15 sts.
**Row 4** K6, yo, p2tog, k5, yo, p2tog—15 sts.
**Row 5** Yo, p2tog, ssk, k1, k2tog, yo, k2tog, k6—13 sts.
**Row 6** Bind off 3 sts, k2, yo, p2tog, SK2P, yo, p2tog—8 sts.

### Acorn Insert
Cast on 9 sts.
**Row 1** *[Yo, p2tog] twice, (k1, p1, k1, p1, k1) in next st, [yo, p2tog] twice—13 sts.
**Rows 2–4** *[Yo, p2tog] twice, k5, [yo, p2tog] twice.
**Row 5** [Yo, p2tog] twice, ssk, k1, k2tog, [yo, p2tog] twice—11 sts.
**Row 6** [Yo, P2tog] twice, SK2P, [yo, P2tog] twice—9 sts.

## NOTES

**1)** The front and back are each worked in 5 parts with 4 additional insertions for the neckline. The sleeves are worked in 4 parts.

**2)** For the front and back, make certain that the "Acorns" in the 2 insertions and at the base of the neck are pointed in the same direction when the garment is seamed. For the sleeves, make certain that the "Acorns" in the bottom edging and those in the elbow insertion are pointed in the same direction when the sleeves are seamed and that the sleeve edgings and insertion Acorns are pointed in the same direction as those on the insertions for the front and back.

## BACK

### Panel 1

With circular needle(s), cast on 290 (314, 358) sts. Work in lacy knots pat as foll:

**Row 1 (RS)** K1 (selvage st), work 0 (4, 2) sts in St st, work 16-st rep 18 (19, 22) times, work 0 (4, 2) sts in St st, k1 (selvage st). Cont in pat until rows 1–16 have been worked 3 times, then rep rows 1–6 once more.

**Dec row 1 (RS)** K1, *k2tog; rep from * to last st, k1—146 (158, 180) sts.

**Dec row 2 (WS)** K1, *p2tog; rep from * to last st, k1—74 (80, 91) sts.

Bind off. Piece should measure approx 8"/20.5cm from beg.

### Insert 1

With straight needles, cast on 9 sts and work 25 (27, 31) reps of 6-row acorn insert.

Piece should measure 2¼"/5.5cm wide and approx 24 (26, 29½)"/61 (66, 75)cm long. Bind off. Sew side edge of insert to top bound-off edge of panel 1.

### Insert 2

With straight needles, cast on 9 sts and work 14 (15, 16) reps of 6-row acorn insertion pat. Bind off. Piece should measure approx 13½ (14½, 15½)"/34 (37, 39.5)cm long.

### BODICE

Pick up 66 (74, 82) sts evenly across top edge of insert 2 as foll:

### For Size Small Only

Skip 3rd space, then every 4th space 5 times, then every 5th space 12 times.

### For Size Medium Only

Skip 4th space, then every 5th space 5 times, then every 6th space 10 times.

### For Size Large Only

Skip 6th space 3 times, then every 7th space 11 times.

### For All Sizes

Work in lacy knots pat as foll:

**Row 1 (RS)** K1 (selvage st), work 0 (4, 0) sts in St st, work 16-st rep 4 (4, 5) times, work 0 (4, 0) sts in St st, k1 (selvage st). Cont in pat, inc 1 st each side (working inc sts into pat) every other row 7 times, then every 3rd row twice—84 (92, 100) sts. Work even until piece measures 4¾"/11.5cm above pick-up row, end with WS row.

### Armhole and Neck Shaping

Bind off 2 (3, 3) sts at beg of next 4 (2, 4) rows, 1 (2, 2) sts at beg of next 6 (4, 4) rows, 0 (1, 1) st at beg of next 0 (6, 4) rows—70 (72, 76) sts.
Work even until armhole measures 4¾ (5¼, 5¾)"/12 (13.5, 14.5)cm.

### Neck Shaping

**Next row (RS)** Work 7 (8, 10) sts, join 2nd ball of yarn and bind off center 56 sts, work to end. Work both sides at once until armhole measures 7 (7½, 8)"/17.5 (19, 20.5)cm. Place all sts on a holder.

## FRONT

Work as for back until bodice measures 4½ (4¾, 5¼)"/10.5 (12, 13.5) cm above the pick-up row, end with WS row.

**Note** For size Small, armhole shaping begins after neck shaping, for sizes Medium and Large, armhole shaping begins before neck shaping.

### Neck Shaping

Cont armhole shaping (if necessary) and bind off center 56 sts for neck and complete as for back.

## PANEL #2

(make 1 for front, 1 for back)

With RS facing, pick up 66 (74, 82) sts along opposite edge of insert 2 same as for Bodice. Work lacy knots pat in reverse (from row 16 to row 1) as foll:

**Row 16 of pat (WS)** Purl.

**Next (inc) row (row 15 of pat) (RS)** *[K in front and back of next st] 3 (3, 4) times, k1; rep from * 9 (17, 7) times more, **[k in front and back of next st] 2 (0, 3) times, k1 (0, 1); rep from ** 7 (0, 9) times more, [k in front and back of next st] twice—114 (130, 146) sts.

**Row 14 of pat** Purl.

**Row 13 of pat (RS)** K1 (selvage st), work 16-st rep 7 (8, 9) times, k1 (selvage st).

Cont in pat as established and work in reverse until 56 rows of pat have been worked. Bind off.

## SLEEVES

With straight needles cast on 8 sts for lower edge and work 6 rows of acorn edging 16 (16, 18) times. Piece should measure

approx 16 (16, 18)"/40.5 (40.5, 45.5)cm. Bind off.
Pick up 82 (82, 90) sts along top of edging as foll:

For Sizes Small and Medium Only
Skip 5th row space, then every foll 7th space 12 times, then
every 6th space once—82 sts.

For Size Large Only
Skip 4th row space, then every 5th space 17 times—90 sts.

For All Sizes
Work in St St for 5 rows. Cont in lacy knot pat as foll:
**Row 1 (RS)** K1 (selvage st), work 0 (0, 4) sts in St st, work 16-
st rep 5 times, work 0 (0, 4) sts in St st, k1 (selvage st).
Cont in pat until rows 1–16 have been worked 3 times, then rep
rows 1–6 once more.

For Size Small Only
**Next row (RS)** [K2tog] 7 times, [k1, k2tog] 9 times, [k2tog]
7 times, [k1, k2tog] 9 times—50 sts. Bind off.

For Size Medium Only
**Next row (RS)** [K1, k2tog] 11 times, [k2, k2tog] 4 times,
[k1, k2tog] 11 times—56 sts. Bind off.

For Size Large Only
**Next row (RS)** [K1, k2tog] 30 times—60 sts. Bind off.

Sleeve Insert
With straight needles, cast on 9 sts and work 6 rows of acorn
insert 10 (11, 12) times. Bind off.

Upper Arm
Pick up 50 (56, 60) sts along top of insert as foll:

For size Small only
Skip 5th space, then every 6th space 3 times, then every 7th
space 6 times—50 sts.

For size Medium only
Skip 5th space, then every 6th space 9 times—56 sts.

For size Large only
Skip 5th space, then every 6th space 11 times—60 sts.

Shaping (All Sizes)
Work in lacy knots pat as foll:
**Row 1 (RS)** K1 (selvage st), work 0 (3, 5) sts in St st, work
16-st rep 3 times, work 0 (3, 5) sts in St st, k1 (selvage st).
To mirror pat so it lines up with body, beg pat as foll:

Purl across first WS row, then on next RS row beg working lacy knots pat with row 11 (9, 9) for right sleeve, row 3 (1, 1) for left sleeve. Inc 1 st each side every 3rd row twice, then every 4th row 3 times—60 (66, 70) sts.

Work even for 6 rows more. Piece should measure approx 3½"/9cm from picked-up row.

Cap shaping

**Note** Cap shaping begins on row 11 (9, 9) of 2nd rep for right sleeve and row 3 (9, 9) of 2nd rep for left sleeve. Bind off 3 sts at beg of next 2 rows, 2 sts at beg of next 2 (4, 4) rows, 1 st at beg of next 6 rows, 2 sts at beg of next 2 rows, 1 st at beg of next 2 rows, 2 sts at beg of next 2 rows, 1 st at beg of next 8 (10, 12) rows, 3 sts at beg of next 4 rows. Bind off rem 14 (14, 16) sts.

Neck Border

Make two 11-rep acorn inserts for base of front and back neck opening, and two 5-rep inserts for sides of neck.

Finishing

Block pieces to measurements.

Slip shoulder stitches from holders back onto needles. Using 3-needle bind-off (see page 164), seam shoulders.

Sew two 11-rep neck border acorn inserts widthwise along front and back necklines.

Sew two 5-rep neck border acorn inserts along sides of neck as foll:

First sew them horizontally at each edge along tops of 11-rep inserts, then sew them vertically along sides of neck.

Sew panel 2 to top of acorn insert 1. It has been seamed to top of panel 1 on back and front.

Sew side seams.

Sew bottom of sleeve to base of 10 (11, 12) rep acorn insert.

Seam, then set in sleeves, placing 3 knots running on a diagonal at edge of caps along seams of both fronts.●

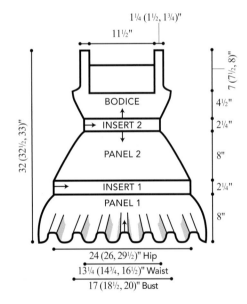

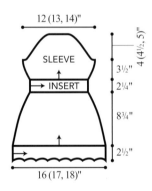

↑ = Direction of work

# HELPFUL INFORMATION

## Standard Yarn Weight System

**Categories of yarn, gauge ranges, and recommended needle and hook sizes**

| Yarn Weight Symbol & Category | 0 Lace | 1 Super Fine | 2 Fine | 3 Light | 4 Medium | 5 Bulky | 6 Super Bulky | 7 Jumbo |
|---|---|---|---|---|---|---|---|---|
| Type of Yarns in Category | Fingering 10-count crochet thread | Sock, Fingering, Baby | Sport, Baby | DK, Light Worsted | Worsted, Afghan, Aran | Chunky, Craft, Rug | Super Bulky, Roving | Jumbo, Roving |
| Knit Gauge Range* in Stockinette Stitch to 4 inches | 33–40** sts | 27–32 sts | 23–26 sts | 21–24 sts | 16–20 sts | 12–15 sts | 7–11 sts | 6 sts and fewer |
| Recommended Needle in Metric Size Range | 1.5–2.25 mm | 2.25—3.25 mm | 3.25—3.75 mm | 3.75—4.5 mm | 4.5—5.5 mm | 5.5—8 mm | 8—12.75 mm | 12.75 mm and larger |
| Recommended Needle U.S. Size Range | 000–1 | 1 to 3 | 3 to 5 | 5 to 7 | 7 to 9 | 9 to 11 | 11 to 17 | 17 and larger |
| Crochet Gauge* Ranges in Single Crochet to 4 inch | 32–42 double crochets** | 21–32 sts | 16–20 sts | 12–17 sts | 11–14 sts | 8–11 sts | 6–9 sts | 5 sts and fewer |
| Recommended Hook in Metric Size Range | Steel*** 1.6–1.4 mm | 2.25—3.5 mm | 3.5—4.5 mm | 4.5—5.5 mm | 5.5—6.5 mm | 6.5—9 mm | 9—16 mm | 16 mm and larger |
| Recommended Hook U.S. Size Range | Steel*** 6, 7, 8 Regular hook B–1 | B–1 to E–4 | E–4 to 7 | 7 to I–9 | I–9 to K–10 1/2 | K–10 1/2 to M–13 | M–13 to Q | Q and larger |

\* GUIDELINES ONLY: The above reflect the most commonly used gauges and needle or hook sizes for specific yarn categories.

\*\* Lace weight yarns are usually knitted or crocheted on larger needles and hooks to create lacy, openwork patterns. Accordingly, a gauge range is difficult to determine. Always follow the gauge stated in your pattern.

\*\*\* Steel crochet hooks are sized differently from regular hooks—the higher the number, the smaller the hook, which is the reverse of regular hook sizing

This Standards & Guidelines booklet and downloadable symbol artwork are available at: **YarnStandards.com**

## RESOURCES

Ancient Arts Fibre Crafts
www.ancientartsfibre.com

Anny Blatt
www.annyblattnorthamerica.com

Anzula Luxury Fibers
www.anzula.com

Artyarns
www.artyarns.com

Bergère de France
www.bergeredefrance.com

Berroco
www.berroco.com

Cascade Yarns
www.cascadeyarns.com

Debbie Bliss
www.debbieblissonline.com

Halcyon Yarn
www.halcyonyarn.com

Hikoo/Skacel Collection, Inc.
www.skacelknitting.com

Jade Sapphire Exotic Fibres
www.jadesapphire.com

Katia
www.katia.com

Kelbourne Woolens
www.kelbournewoolens.com

Koigu
www.koigu.com

Lana Grossa
www.lana-grossa.de/en

Lorna's Laces
www.lornaslaces.net

Madelinetosh
www.madelinetosh.com

Malabrigo
www.malabrigoyarn.com

Manos del Uruguay
www.manos.uy

Rowan
www.knitrowan.com

Squoosh Fiberarts
www.squooshfiberarts.com

String Yarns
www.stringyarns.com

Tahki Stacy Charles
www.tahkistacycharles.com

Trendsetter Yarn Group
www.trendsetteryarns.com

Universal Yarn
www.universalyarn.com

WEBS
www.yarn.com

Willow Yarns
www.willowyarns.com

Yarnspirations
www.yarnspirations.com

Zealana
www.zealana.com

## ABBREVIATIONS

| | |
|---|---|
| **2nd** | second |
| **approx** | approximately |
| **beg** | begin(ning) |
| **CC** | contrasting color |
| **ch** | chain |
| **cm** | centimeter(s) |
| **cn** | cable needle |
| **cont** | continu(e)(ing) |
| **dec** | decreas(e)(es)(ing) |
| **dec'd** | decreased |
| **dpn** | double-pointed needle(s) |
| **foll** | follow(s)(ing) |
| **g** | gram(s) |
| **inc** | increas(e)(es)(ing) |
| **inc'd** | increased |
| **k** | knit |
| **kfb** | knit into the front and back of a stitch—1 knit stitch increased |
| **k2tog** | knit 2 stitches together—1 stitch decreased |
| **k3tog** | knit 3 stitches together—2 stitches decreased |
| **LH** | left-hand |
| **lp(s)** | loop(s) |
| **m** | meter(s) |
| **M1(L)** | Insert LH needle from front to back under strand between last st worked and next st on LH needle, knit strand through back loop—1 knit stitch increased. |
| **M1 p-st** | Insert LH needle from front to back under strand between last st worked and next st on LH needle, purl strand through back loop—1 purl stitch increased. |
| **M1R** | Insert tip of LH needle from back to front under strand between last st worked and next st on LH needle, knit strand through front loop—1 stitch increased |
| **MC** | main color |
| **mm** | millimeter(s) |
| **oz** | ounce(s) |
| **p** | purl |
| **p2tog** | purl 2 stitches together—1 stitch decreased |
| **pat(s)** | pattern(s) |
| **pm** | place marker |

| | |
|---|---|
| **psso** | pass slip stitch(es) over |
| **rem** | remain(s)(ing) |
| **rep** | repeat |
| **rev** | reverse |
| **RH** | right-hand |
| **rnd(s)** | round(s) |
| **RS** | right side(s) |
| **S2KP** | slip 2 stitches together knitwise, knit 1, pass 2 slipped stitches over knit stitch—2 stitches decreased |
| **sc** | single crochet |
| **SKP** | slip 1 stitch, knit 1 stitch, pass slipped stitch over—1 stitch decreased |
| **SK2P** | slip 1 stitch, knit 2 stitches together, pass slipped stitch over 2 stitches knit together—2 stitches decreased |
| **sl** | slip |
| **sl st** | slip stitch |
| **sm** | slip marker |
| **ssk** | slip next 2 stitches knitwise one at a time, return slipped stitches to left-hand needle, knit these 2 stitches together—1 stitch decreased |
| **ssp** | slip next 2 stitches purlwise one at a time, return slipped stitches to left-hand needle, purl these 2 stitches together—1 stitch decreased |
| **sssk** | slip next 3 stitches knitwise one at a time, insert tip of LH needle into fronts of these stitches and knit them together—2 stitches decreased |
| **st(s)** | stitch(es) |
| **St st** | stockinette stitch |
| **tbl** | through back loop(s) |
| **tog** | together |
| **w&t** | wrap and turn |
| **WS** | wrong side(s) |
| **wyib** | with yarn in back |
| **wyif** | with yarn in front |
| **yd** | yard(s) |
| **yo** | yarn over |
| **\*** | repeat directions following * as many times as indicated |
| **[ ]** | repeat directions inside brackets as many times as indicated |

## SKILL LEVELS

**BASIC**
Projects using basic stitches.
May include basic increases and decreases.

**EASY**
Projects may include simple stitch patterns, colorwork, and/or shaping.

**INTERMEDIATE**
Projects may include involved stitch patterns, colorwork, and/or shaping.

**COMPLEX**
Projects may include complex stitch patterns, colorwork, and/or shaping using a variety of techniques and stitches simultaneously.

## KNITTING NEEDLE SIZES

| US | Metric |
|---|---|
| 0 | 2mm |
| 1 | 2.25mm |
| 2 | 2.75mm |
| 3 | 3.25mm |
| 4 | 3.5mm |
| 5 | 3.75mm |
| 6 | 4mm |
| 7 | 4.5mm |
| 8 | 5mm |
| 9 | 5.5mm |
| 10 | 6mm |
| 10½ | 6.5mm |
| 11 | 8mm |
| 13 | 9mm |
| 15 | 10mm |
| 17 | 12.75mm |
| 19 | 15mm |
| 35 | 19mm |

# TECHNIQUES

## KITCHENER STITCH

Cut a tail at least 4 times the length of the edge that will be grafted together and thread through a tapestry needle. Hold needles together with right sides showing, making sure each has the same number of live stitches, and work as follows:

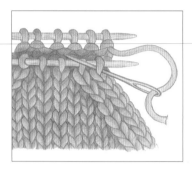

**1)** Insert tapestry needle purlwise through first stitch on front needle. Pull yarn through, leaving stitch on needle.

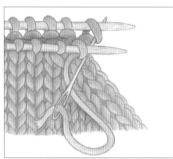

**2)** Insert tapestry needle knitwise through first stitch on back needle. Pull yarn through, leaving stitch on needle.

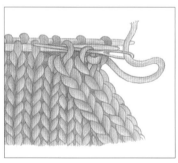

**3)** Insert tapestry needle knitwise through first stitch on front needle, pull yarn through, and slip stitch off needle. Then, insert tapestry needle purlwise through next stitch on front needle and pull yarn through, leaving this stitch on needle.

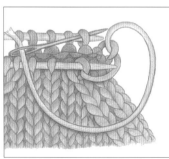

**4)** Insert tapestry needle purlwise through first stitch on back needle, pull yarn through, and slip stitch off needle. Then, insert tapestry needle knitwise through next stitch on back needle and pull yarn through, leaving this stitch on needle.

Repeat steps 3 and 4 until all stitches on front and back needles have been grafted.

## 3-NEEDLE BIND-OFF

**1)** With the right sides of the two pieces facing each other, and the needles held parallel, insert a third needle knitwise into the first stitch of each needle and wrap the yarn around the needle as if to knit.

**2)** Knit these 2 stitches together and slip them off the needles. *Knit the next 2 stitches together in the same way as shown.

**3)** Slip the first stitch on the third needle over the second stitch and off the needle.

Repeat from the * in step 2 across the row until all the stitches are bound off.

## PROVISIONAL CAST-ON

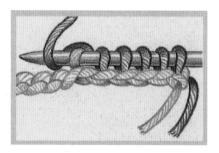

With scrap yarn and crochet hook, chain the number of stitches to cast on, plus a few extra. Cut a tail and pull the tail through the last chain stitch. With knitting needle and yarn, pick up and knit the stated number of stitches through the "purl bumps" on the back of the chain. To remove scrap chain, when instructed, pull out the tail from the last crochet stitch. Gently and slowly pull on the tail to unravel the crochet stitches, carefully placing each released knit stitch on a needle.

## HALF DOUBLE CROCHET (HDC)

**1)** With crochet hook in a loop connected to your work, make a yarnover.

**2)** Insert the hook into the next stitch and yarn over again.

**3)** Draw the yarn over through the stitch—you now have 3 loops on the hook—and then yarn over once more.

**4)** Draw the last yarnover through all 3 loops on hook. You have now completed one half double crochet (hdc) stitch.

## CROCHET SLIP STITCH (SL ST)

**1)** With crochet hook in a loop connected to your work, insert the hook into the next stitch and yarn over.

**2)** Draw the yarnover through the stitch and then through the loop on the hook in one movement. You have completed one slip stitch (sl st).

## SINGLE CROCHET (SC)

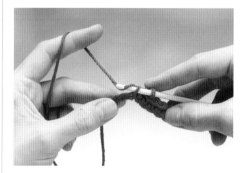

**1)** Insert the hook into the next stitch. Make a yarnover and catch it on the hook.

**2)** Pull the hook through the stitch—you now have two loops on the hook—then yarn over again.

**3)** Draw the yarnover through both loops on the hook. You have now completed one single crochet (sc) stitch.

# INDEX

# Build Your VOGUE KNITTING Collection

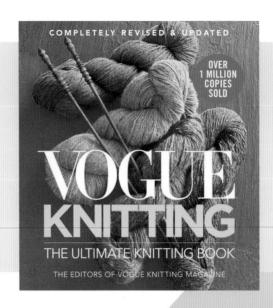

COMPLETELY REVISED & UPDATED

OVER 1 MILLION COPIES SOLD

## VOGUE KNITTING
### THE ULTIMATE KNITTING BOOK
THE EDITORS OF VOGUE KNITTING MAGAZINE

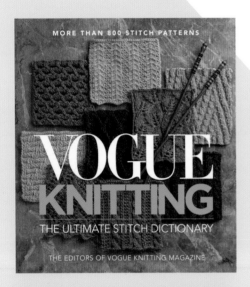

MORE THAN 800 STITCH PATTERNS

## VOGUE KNITTING
### THE ULTIMATE STITCH DICTIONARY
THE EDITORS OF VOGUE KNITTING MAGAZINE

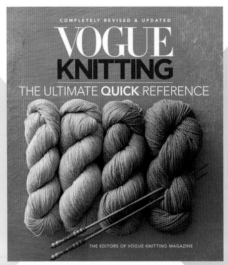

COMPLETELY REVISED & UPDATED

## VOGUE KNITTING
### THE ULTIMATE QUICK REFERENCE
THE EDITORS OF VOGUE KNITTING MAGAZINE

## VOGUE KNITTING
### PROJECT JOURNAL

## VOGUE KNITTING
### THE LEARN-TO-KNIT BOOK
THE EDITORS OF VOGUE KNITTING MAGAZINE

VOGUE KNITTING

## NORAH GAUGHAN
### 40 TIMELESS KNITS
BY THE EDITORS OF VOGUE KNITTING MAGAZINE

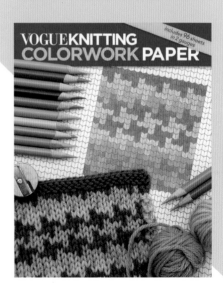

Includes 96 sheets in 2 gauges

## VOGUE KNITTING
### COLORWORK PAPER